The Coding Strategy

for Troubleshooting

신승훈 · 최경희 · 서주영 · 이택균 · 예홍진 · 정기현 지음
Kristin H. Chung 역

Human Science
휴먼싸이언스

정가 25,000원

The Coding Strategy for Troubleshooting

2016년 8월 20일 초판 인쇄
2016년 8월 31일 초판 발행

저　　자 : 신 승 훈 외 5
역　　자 : Kristin H. Chung
발 행 자 : 박　주　옥
발 행 처 : 휴먼싸이언스
주　　소 : 서울시 도봉구 시루봉로 291 B1
(도봉동 613-14 숙진빌딩)
등록번호 : 제2008-20호
등 록 일 : 2008. 10. 13
전　　화 : (02) 955-0244
팩　　스 : (02) 955-0245
e-mail : humansci@naver.com
I S B N : 978-89-93712-77-3 93560

역자와의 협의하에 인지생략

Preface

We are living in the world where all leaders and governments think that the software education is needed for everyone for the development of their states. Software education includes the ethics and knowledge needed to solve the facing problems. It encourages the creative problem solving capability through an integration of human thinking and computational thinking that resulted from the data processing.

Coding is writing a program using a programming language based on the process flow of the tasks that need to be handled by the computer. To be equipped with good coding capability, a student should understand how the computer handles the data, learn certain computer programming language, and especially be able to personally write a "good" program that executes on the computer.

Coding is one of the most difficult area for the university students who are interested in the computer science. It is not easy to start writing a program of a given problem even after students understood the problem and learned the program language. Further more students question about the quality of their program and wonder whether they spent too much time and efforts for the program they successfully executed.

This is the reason why we decided to write this book. If the coding capability is one of the mandatory skill that all students need to learn like Mathematics or English class, then we need a self-study textbook that guides the students to easily learn the needed skills by themselves.

Instead of introducing the grammar and syntax of the certain program language like C or C++, this book guides direction for students to understand and to analyze the given problem, and also to focuses on the hands-on-practices of writing a good program through the example code.

Simply states, coding is written by a human being with a language that a computer understands and is executed by a computer. People need the coding strategies to solve the problems with computer program like we need a good skill to handle a machine efficiently. Programming requires very complicated and abstracted thinking ability to make decisions on choosing appropriate data structure, data analysis method, algorithms that solves the problem from many alternatives and also that always provides correct results.

It is a good studying method to follow a good example program that can be found from the other books or the open-source code. In this case, it is important to think about why the author coded the program this way instead of just copying the code. It is illegal and plagiarism to copy the entire code written by other people without permission since the software is copyright protected. We can be punished by the law if we violate the copyright.

There are 25 projects in this book. Each project includes main concepts, main objectives, and lab practices to solve the project problem. The prepared source code per project will be given to the students so they do not loose the objectives of the program design. KeyPoints section of the textbook further helps students to understand more clearly on the tasks needed to be performed to solve the project problem.

It is recommended to give enough study time depending on the level of the computer knowledge of the student and the teaching method. It is expected for a student to spend 1 to 3 hours to solve a project assignment depending on the difficulty level of the problem, but it can take longer for some students. It might take 45 hours to 90 hours of student's time to solve all projects. It is also very important to follow the order of the projects in the textbook since it is layed out so that it is closely related to the suggested order of learning the coding strategy for troubleshooting. Do not arbitrarily change the order of the projects simply to manage or to save time, or to encourage student's interests.

We give special thanks to publishing company partakers who have provided uncountable help and encouragements and also to those students who became subject of experiment of lab projects for past few years regardless of their intension.

2015, February
Authors

Contents

The Coding Strategy
for Troubleshooting

Project 00

The Coding Strategy for Troubleshooting

Creating C Program with Visual Studio

Project Description

Creating C/C++ Project with Visual Studio

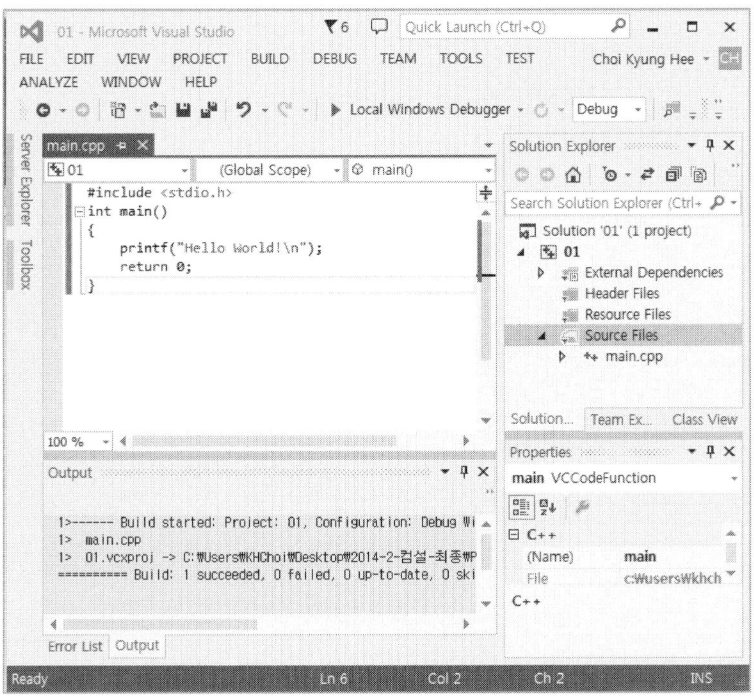

Main Concepts

IDE

- IDE(Integrated Development Environment)
  The software supporting the functionality to develop the program
- Visual Studio 2013
  IDE developed by Microsoft at 2013

Project

- Project
  - ✓ A collection of everything (source code and resource) related to the program
  - ✓ In order to make a program using Visual Studio, you must create a project first

Main Objectives

✎ Creating project with Visual Studio
✎ Coding simple program using C language

00.01 Executing and Examining Visual Studio

Practice

✻ Execute Visual Studio

- Double-click Visual Studio icon in desktop
- Window's 'Start menu' > Double-click 'Visual Studio 2013'
- Window's 'Start menu' > 'All programs' > 'Visual Studio 2013' > Double-click 'Visual Studio 2013'

✻ Examine Visual Studio Interface Configuration

- Visual Studio Menu
- Solution Explorer, etc.

✻ Explore Functionality

- Observe all results after left-clicking every menu and submenu

KeyPoints

+ Type/Functionality of click

- left-click /Selection
- right-click /Exploration
- double-click /Execution

Output

00.02 Creating Project

Practice

※ Execute Menu ('File' > 'New')

※ Follow the procedures below after the dialog appears

- Programming language : C++
- Application program type : Win32 console application program
- Project save folder : 'Ajou' folder in desktop (Create 'Ajou' folder in desktop beforehand)
- Project name : JustPrint
- Click 'Confirm' button

※ Click 'Next' button after 'Application program wizard' appears

※ Follow the steps below after showing 'Application program wizard' appears

- Application program type : "Console application program"
- Additional option : "Empty project"
- Click 'Finish' button

KeyPoints

+ Precaution

- Set different options depending on program type and language
- Examine how it is created

Output

00.03 Completing Project(Programming with C)

Practice

※ Check Project Creation

- Check 'JustPrint' folder in project save folder 'Ajou'

※ Check Solution Explorer in Visual Studio window

- Control the menu to show solution explorer
  - Menu 'View' > 'Solution Explorer'

※ Add program source file main.cpp as new item

- Right-click 'Source file' of solution explorer
- Select 'Add' > 'New item' on **Context Menu** after right-clicking
- Select 'C++ file' after dialog appears
- Input main.cpp in 'File name' field and click 'Add' button
- Check the change of solution explorer

※ Coding main.cpp with C language

- Double-click 'main.cpp' item in solution explorer
- Write a code below to the code editor window in the middle

```
#include <stdio.h>
int main(void)
{
   printf("Hello\n");
   printf("My First Program\n");
   return 0;
}
```

- Scan typographical errors

KeyPoints

+ Project Folder

Folder containing project related items

+ Item

Project elements (Source file, Header file, Resource file)

Output

00.04 Executing Program

Practice

✻ Execute program

- Press Ctrl Key(Left bottom side) and F5 Key(The upper side) in the keyboard(Ctrl+F5)
- Check execution result in Console window

✻ Edit and execute program

- Change string "Hello" to your name
  - If your name is "Smith", change `printf("Smith\n");`
- Execute program with Ctrl+F5
- Check execution result in Console window

✻ Save current project

- Execute save menu
- Check main.cpp in project folder

✻ Terminate Visual Studio

- Execute terminate menu

KeyPoints

- Keep an eye on file name in project folder
- String
  A set of characters in " "
- ₩ means backslash (\) in '₩n'

Output

Project **01** The Coding Strategy for Troubleshooting

Executing and Debugging C Program

Project Description

Executing and Debugging C Program

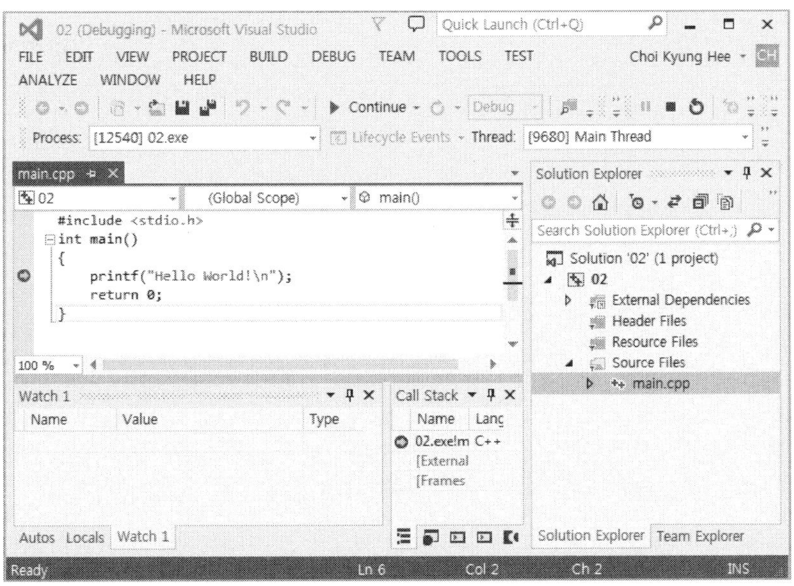

Main Concepts

Bugs

If the program makes wrong and unexpected outputs, we can say that there is a bug.

Ref. Bug means 'insect' in English

Debugging

- Debugging

  The process of finding and fixing the bugs in the program

- Debugger

  Software that supports debugging

Main Objectives

- Operating project
- Dealing with various errors
- Reviewing and executing the program
- Learn debugging

01.01 Open project and error handling

Practice

※ Open project

- Execute Visual Studio
- Execute menu
  ('File' > 'Open' > 'Project/Solution')
- Select project in file explorer

※ Error handling

- C syntax error
  - Delete '>' in #include <stdio.h>, or
  - Delete ')' in int main(void)
- Build failure
  - Click 'No' button if Visual Studio asks to execute previous version when error occurs
  - Check error point and cause in the bottom of Visual Studio
  - Fix code
- Logic error
  - Program is executed but the output is wrong (e.g. the expected output is 100, but 99 is output)
  - Analyze code in detail

KeyPoints

+ Syntax error
- Error resulting from wrong C syntax

+ Build
- Creating a executable program(.exe file)
- After build, the program can be executed

+ Bug type/ debugging
- Syntax error/easy
- Logic error/difficult

Output

01.02 Using debugger

Practice

※ Re-write main.cpp of the project with the following code

```
#include <stdio.h>
int main(void)
{
   int  a;
   int  b;
   a =1;
   b =a+1;
   printf("a+b=%d\n",a+b);
   return 0;
}
```

※ Push Ctrl+F5 and check output

※ Execute debugger

- Set break point at `int a;`
  Left-click certain part in side bar, then break point is indicated by red ball
- Push F5 to execute debugger
  Not Ctrl keypad, but F5 keypad
- Whenever F10 is pushed, it executes the current command and move to the next command
- Putting the mouse pointer over a or b of the executed command for a while shows the value of a or b
- Repeat debugging until you select stop (debugger stop) in menu

KeyPoints

+ Break point
- The command that is temporally stopped and in wait state
- Move to next break point after push F5

+ side bar
- Left-side of source code

+ Debugger shortcut
- F5 : Execute the commands until next break point
- F10 : Execute the next command

Output

Project 02

First Project (Hello World Printing)

Project Description

Write a program that outputs "Hello World!" using the C language. The following is the expected output.

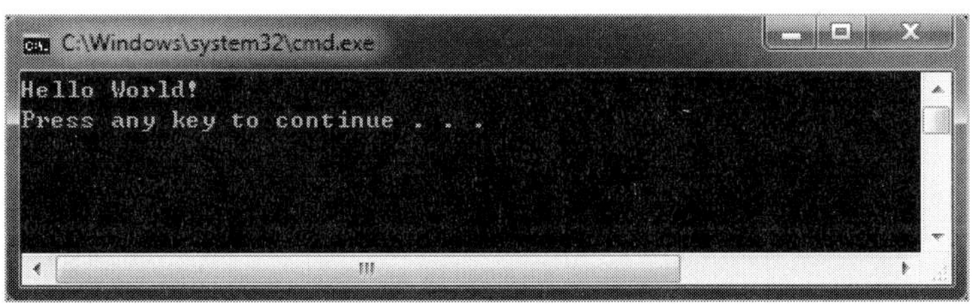

Main Concepts

String : A set of character(char) between double quote(") like "Hello World!" is called a string.

Program : A set of commands described by programming language such as C, C++, Java etc.

Main Objectives

- Review creating project using visual studio
- Structure of C program and `main()` function
- Executing program

02.01 Creating project

◎ Window of Visual Studio 2013 when opened

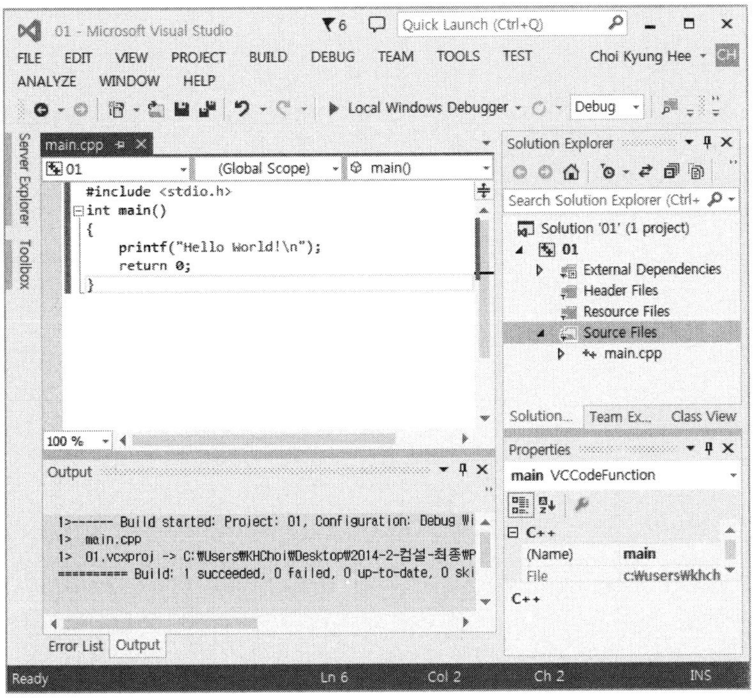

Main Structure of Window

(1) Menu

(2) Solution Explorer

- External Dependencies
- Header Files
- Resource Files
- Source Files

(3) Coding Area (Editing Window)

(4) Message Window

Practice

✻ Program development and execution

✻ Creating project

- Execute Menu('File' > 'New' > 'Project') and Follow the steps below
  - Select 'win32 Console Application Program'
  - Select project folder, input the project name and click 'OK' button
  - Select 'Console Application Program' -> 'Empty Project' and click 'finish' button

✻ `main()` coding

- Add main.cpp as new item to source file of solution explorer
  - Right click -> 'Add' -> 'New item' -> 'C++ file'
  - Input 'main.cpp' to file name filed
- Write commands to the code edit window of main.cpp

✻ Execution

- Push Ctrl+F5
- Check output
- Edit String "Hello World!" to "Hello My Friend!" and Execute

KeyPoints

+ Coding

- Write a program using programming language
- Written program is called source code

+ Ctrl+F5

- Press F5 key while press Ctrl Key
- Used to execute program in Visual Studio

Output

02.02 Understanding Structure of C Program and C Language Syntax

Basic Structure of C Program and Syntax

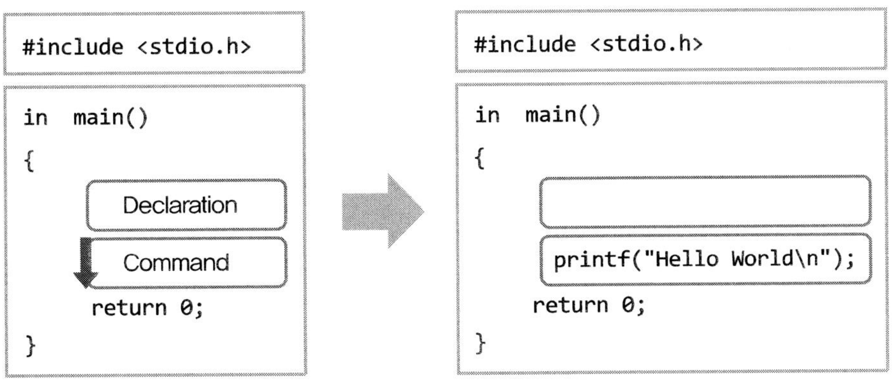

Practice

Understanding C Program

※ Edit code with following steps and execute (Understanding C Language Syntax)

- Edit `#include <stdio.h>` to `/*#include <stdio.h>*/`
- Edit `main(void)` to `mymain(void)`
- Delete `()` in `printf()`
- Delete `";"` in `printf()`

KeyPoints

+ **C Language Syntax**

  is very strict

  - Error occurs when ; , (is missing

Output

Practice

※ Edit code with following steps and execute (Understanding the execution order)

- Write `printf` statement to output your name
  ```
  printf("Hello World\n");
  printf("Smith\n");
  ```
- Delete `\n` in `printf("Hello World\n");`
- Add `\n` like `printf("Hello World\n\n\n");`
- Swap the order of Hello World `printf` statement and your name `printf` statement

※ Meaning of return command

- Put `return;` above of `printf("Smith\n");`
- Put `return;` before `printf("Hello World\n");`

KeyPoints

+ The execution order

- Start at main( )
- Execute from first command
- One by one

+ printf( )

- Outputs on display

+ return 0;

- If you execute return in main(), it terminate the program

Output

02.03 Understanding #define

Defining macro using `#define`

When `#define` MESSAGE `"Hello World\n"`

- `printf(MESSAGE);` is same with `printf("Hello World\n");`
- `MESSAGE` is replaced with `"Hello World\n"`
- `printf("MESSAGE");` is different with `printf("Hello World\n")`

Practice

Edit code with following steps and execute

✻ Define macro

- Add `#define MESSAGE "Hello World\n"` above `main(void)`

✻ Edit code with following steps and execute

- Edit `printf("Hello World\n");` to `printf(MESSAGE);`
- Call `printf(MESSAGE);` three times
- Edit `printf(MESSAGE);` to `printf(message);`
  (Use message instead of MESSAGE)
- Edit `printf(MESSAGE);` to `printf("MESSAGE");`
- Restore to `printf(MESSAGE);` and swap the position of `#include` and `#define`
- Make `#define MESSAGE "…"` to comment

Output

KeyPoints

+ Macro
- General form
  #define A B
- A is replaced with B
- Help coding to be simple

+ Identifier
- Has to be declared before use

+ Distinguishing lower and upper case
- The C language can distinguish lower and upper letters. Therefore, A is different with a

+ Comment
- // : only for target line
- Between /* and */

GUESS??

1) How does programming skill affect major studies in the upper-class?

2) Is a monitor always an output device? Is there any way to use monitor as input device?

3) What is the first step of programming?

4) What are the example of programming language? Which language is used to solve certain problem? Are web programs also written in C language? What language is used to develop Android application?

5) Can you become a great programmer? What attitude is essential to enjoy programming?

6) Edit the followings to a command that does not use macro

(1)

```
#define PRINT printf
PRINT("Hello World!");
```

(2)

```
#define RETURN return
RETURN 0;
```

Project 03

Comparing Two Integers

Project Description

Between the integer 1 and 8, write a program that finds the largest integer and outputs the largest integer 8 as "8 is the largest integer". Following is the expected output.

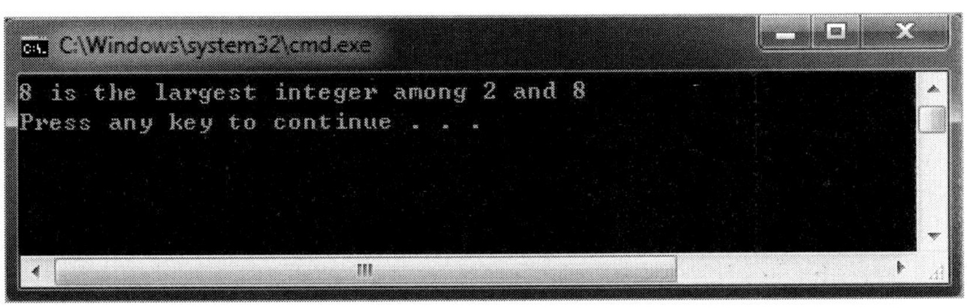

Main Concepts

Integer

- Numbers like −3, −2, −1, 0, 1, 2, 3, ... etc. are called integers
- Two's complement is one method of represent negative number, and the two's complement of N-bit number a is 2^N - a
  - ✓ If N = 4, two's complement of 4-bit number 0100 (decimal number is 4) is 1100, which is 2^4(10000) - 0100
  - ✓ 1100 should not be interpreted as 12, but −4

Variable/Constant

- Variable

  Value can change during program execution

- Constant

  Value cannot change during program execution (0, −2, etc.)

Main Objectives

- ✎ Review creating project
- ✎ Meaning, declaration and type of variables
- ✎ Utilize `#define`
- ✎ Integer value, character value('a', 'A', '1', '2', etc.)

03.01 Review creating project

Program structure model that uses variables

```
#include <stdio.h>

in  main()
{
        Declaration

        Command

        return 0;
}
```

```
#include <stdio.h>
#define MAX2(a.b) ( ((a)>(b))?(a):(b) )

in  main()
{
        int  vOne, vTwo;
        int  vLarqest:

        vOne = 2; vTwo=8;
        vLargest = MAX2(vOne, vTwo);
        printf("%d is the largest integer among %d and %d\n", vLargest,

    return 0;
}
```

Practice

Program development and execution

✻ Creating project

- Select menu('File' > 'New' > 'Project') and follow the step below
  - Select 'win32 Console Application Program'
  - Select project folder, input the project name and click 'OK' button
  - Select 'Console Application Program' -> 'Empty Project' and click 'finish' button

Output

Practice

Program development and execution

✻ Coding

- Add main.cpp as new item to source file of solution explorer
  - Right click -> 'Add' -> 'New item' -> 'C++ file'
  - Input 'main.cpp' to file name filed
- Write commands to code edit window of main.cpp

✻ Execution

- Push Ctrl+F5
- Check output
- Edit program to output the largest value from -1 to 4 and Execute
- Edit %d to %5d in `printf` statement and execute

KeyPoints

+ int vOne, vTwo;
- Variable Declaration
- vOne : Variable name
- int : Variable type

+ vOne = 2;
- Assignment
- Change variable value

+ %d
- Used to output integer value in printf statement

Output

03.02 Declaration and use of variable

Practice

Edit the code with following steps and execute

* Variable declaration method

```
▸ int vOne  vTwo;           // Delete ','
▸ int vOne; int vTwo;       // Declare two variables in a line
▸ int vOne;
  int vTwo;                 // Edit to two declaration
```

* Assignment to variable

```
▸ vOne=20, vTwo=10;                     // Edit value
▸ int vOne, vTwo; vOne = 2; vTwo=8;     // This line is modified
  int vOne=2, vTwo=8;                   // to this line
```

* Compare character value and output using %d

```
▸ vOne = 'a'; vTwo ='A';       // Compare alphabets
▸ vOne = '0'; vTwo ='9';       // Compare numeric characters
▸ vOne = '+'; vTwo ='-';       // Compare special characters
```

* Use of real number type variable

```
▸ float vOne, vTwo;            // Edit type to float
▸ float vOne, vTwo;            // Edit type
  printf("%d ....");           // Edit %d to %f
```

KeyPoints

+ **Declaration should end with ';'**

+ **',' between variable names**

+ **Variable declaration and assignment**

int <Variable name> = Value;

+ **Variable type**
  - int : Integer
  - float : Real number

+ **Output type**
  - %d : Integer
  - %f : Real number

+ **ASCII code**

One of code system to represent character like 'a', 'A', '0', '9', '+', '-' using 8-bit

Output

03.03 Utilize #define and Expand Program

Understanding macro

1) Meaning of `#define MAX2(a,b) (((a)>(b)) ? (a) : (b))`
   - `((a)>(b))` is `true` when `(a)` is greater than `(b)`, or `false`
   - The value of `(A ? B : C)` is `B` when `A` is `true`, or `C` when `A` is `false`
   - `(((a)>(b)) ? (a) : (b))` is `(a)` when `(a)` is greater than `(b)`, or equals to `(b)`

2) Macro to find small value
   - `#define MIN2(a,b) ( ((a)<(b)) ? (a) : (b) )`

Practice

Edit program with following steps and execute

* Edit MAX2 macro

- `#define MAX2(a,b) (((a)>(b)):(a)?(b))`
  - Swap '?' and ':'
- `#define MAX2(a,b) (((a)<(b))?(a):(b))`
  - Edit '>' to '<" (Small value is output)
- Edit macro to output small value using MIN2 macro

KeyPoints

+ A?B:C

- Error occur when ? and : are modified or omitted

Output

Practice

Edit program with following steps and execute

※ Expand program to find the largest number among three numbers

- Add new variable for third number

```
int vThree;
vThree = 7;
```

- Refine the way to find the largest number among three numbers
  - (Step 1) Compare vOne and vTwo and save larger number to vLargest

```
vLargest = MAX2(vOne, vTwo);
```

  - (Step 2) Save larger number between vLargest and vThree to vLargest

```
vLargest = MAX2(vLargest, vThree);
```

KeyPoints

+ **Task refinement**
  - Refine one task to a set of subtask

Output

GUESS??

1) Find two's complement of given binary numbers

(1) `1111`

(2) `0001`

(3) `00000001`

(4) `01111111`

2) In the system to represent integer to two's complement, what is the range of expressable numbers using 4-bit?

3) What is the variable type of given variables?

```
int     a;
float   b;
char    c;
double  d;
```

4) What are the variable types used in C language?

5) How many bytes are used to represent each variable type used in C language?

Project 04

The Coding Strategy for Troubleshooting

Solving Linear Equation

Project Description

Write a program that solves linear equation x + 1 = 0 and outputs the root. Following is the expected output.

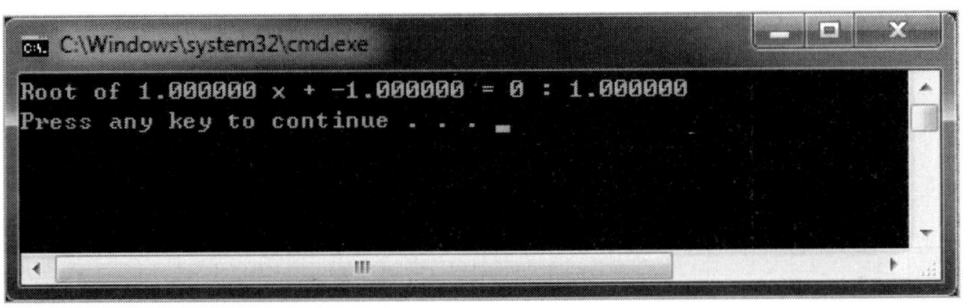

Main Concepts

Floating point(**float**, **double**)

Floating point is a method of representing the real number. The real number is represented using significant digits and exponent. In computer, sign, significant digits and exponent are stored.

<sign> Significant digits × base^{exponent}

If statement

Commands that are chosen based on each condition

- Basic form

```
if (Condition)
    Command A;  // Command A is executed when the condition is true
else
    Command B;  // Command A is executed when the condition is false
```

- Non-else form

```
if (Condition)
    Command A;
// Command A is executed when the condition is true
// When the condition is false, there are no commands
```

Main Objectives

- Simple four fundamental arithmetic calculation
- Influence of variable types on calculations
  (Difference between `int` and `float`)
- Analyzing and handling many different cases(Use of `if`)
- `if` statement

04.01 Review creating project

◎ Design logic of **main()**

```
#include <stdio.h>
int main(void)
{
    float  a, b;
    float  root;
    | Represent equation using a coefficient           |
    | Calculate the root using formula root = -b/a     |
    | Output result                                    |
    return 0;
}
```

Practice

Project completion and coding

✻ Project completion

- After creating project, add main.cpp as new item
- Code main.cpp
- Execute and check output

Output

Practice

※ Text the cases below

- The root of 2 * x - 1 = 0

  `a = 2; b = -1;`
- The root of 0 * x - 1 = 0 (Equation without no root)

  `a = 0; b = -1;`
- The root of 0 * x + 0 = 0 (Equation with countless roots)

  `a = 0; b = 0;`
- `a = 0.0000000000000000000000000000000000000001;`

  `b = 1;`

KeyPoints

+ Real coefficient

- Use float

+ Symbol of operation

- Addition : +
- Subtraction : -
- Multiplication : *
- Division : /

Output

04.02 Influence of variable types on calculations

Practice

Influence of improper type

✻ Influence of type inconsistency

- Edit `float a, b;` to `int a, b;` (Only a and b)

✻ Inconsistency between type and formula

- Edit type of `root` to `int root;` and execute

✻ Consistency between type and `printf` statement

- Edit `%f` of `printf("Root = %f \n",root);` to `%d`
- Find the root of given equations

  2x - 4 = 0

  2x - 3 = 0

  2x - 1 = 0

✻ Diverse output formats

- Edit `%f` to `%.2f` and execute
- Edit `%f` to `%5.1f` and execute
- Edit to `%10.1f` and execute
- Edit to `%010.1f` and execute

KeyPoints

+ printf format

- %d : Integer
- %f : Real number

+ Integer / Integer

- Calculate portion
- 7/2 is 3

+ 7/2 and 7./2 are different

- 7/2 :Integer division
- 7./2:Real number division
- If any of them is real number, there are real type calculation

Output

04.03 Selecting commands based on the condition - if statement

Meaning of **if** statement

```
if(a == 0) {
   if (b == 0) {
        printf("There are countless roots, because a=0 and b=0 \n");
   }
   else {
        printf( "There is no root, because a=0 and b!=0 \n");
   }
}
else {                          // In case that there is a root "-b/a"
   root = -b / a;
   printf("The root of %.2f x + %.2f = 0 : %.2f\n", a, b, root);
}
```

Practice

※ Edit program to handle many different cases

- Edit every variable type to `float` and output format to `%.2f`
- Implement the logic above
- Find the root of given equations
  - (a) 2x - 3 = 0
  - (b) 0x + 1 = 0
  - (c) 0x + 0 = 0
- Find the root after editing `if(a == 0)` to `if(a = 0)`

KeyPoints

+ Condition that a is equal with b

- a == b
- Two '='

Output

Practice

* In order to check the syntax of `if` statement, try to find the root of above equations after following modification
  - Delete '{' in `if (va != 0) {`
  - Delete `else` one by one
  - Edit `if` to `IF`
  - Edit `else` to `ELSE`

KeyPoints

+ { }
- Binding many commands
- No ; after { }
- When the condition is true and there is a single command in the if statement, { } is not necessary
- if(a==0)   return;

Output

GUESS??

1) Because we know the root is 1, what happens is we output `printf("The root = 1.000000\n");` without calculation? If the root is not 1 like $2x - 3 = 0$, is it possible to change the output?

2) Which operations can be used in program?

3) In our daily life, are there the cases like `if` statements where we chose different actions based on the conditions?

Project 05

Solving Quadratic Equation

Project Description

Write a program that finds and outputs two roots of the quadratic equation $x^2 + 2x + 1 = 0$ as seen in following picture.

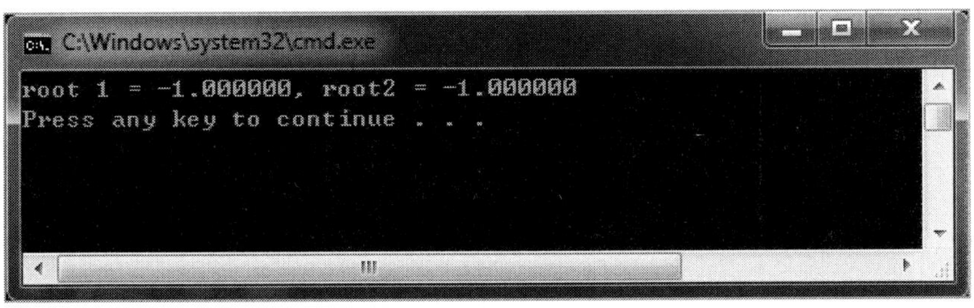

Main Concepts

Formula Expression

- Quadratic Formula

  $(-b \pm \text{Square\_Root}(b^2 - 4ac))/(2a)$

  $\Rightarrow (-b \pm \text{sqrt}(b * b - 4 * a * c))/(2 * a)$

- Function to find square root : `sqrt()`

Main Objectives

- Review creating project and execution procedure
- Handling many different cases(Construct and use of `if` statement)
- Formula expression, mathematical functions like `sqrt()` and header file `<math.h>`

05.01 Create and execute program

main.cpp

```
#include <stdio.h>
#include <math.h>

int main(void)
{
   float a, b, c;
   float root1, root2;

   A commands to find two roots and store them to
   root1 and root2, respectively

   return 0;
}
```

Practice

※ Project completion

- Select menu 'File' > 'New' > 'Project'
- Add main.cpp as new item to 'source file' of solution explorer
- Code main.cpp
  - Note the addition of `#include <math.h>`
- Check that the roots are correct by executing program with Ctrl+F5

※ Header file `#include`

- Make `#include <math.h>` to comment as seen in below and execute

```
//#include <math.h>
```

KeyPoints

+ Header file

- Proper header file requires #include
- Mathematical formular requires <math.h>

Output

05.02 Examine program reaction to various inputs

Practice

* Edit a coefficient of quadratic equation as seen in below and execute
  - `a=1; b=1; c=1;`
  - `a=0; b=1; c=1;`
  - `int a, b, c;`
  - `a=2; b=3; c=1;`
  - `a=1; b=2; c=1;`
* Designate the value output format
  - `%.2f` instead of `%f`
  - `%5.1f` instead of `%f`

KeyPoints

+ sqrt()

- Parameter should be float or double

+ Library

- In addition to sqrt(), there are many functions to find sin x, log x, xy, etc.

+ output format

- %.2f
- Output the value to the second decimal places

Output

05.03 Expand program to find the roots of various quadratic equations

Data Validation Check

```
if (Condition) {
    Executed commands when
    the condition is true
}
else {
    Executed commands when
    the condition is false
}
```

```
if (Condition) {
    root1 = (-b + sqrt(b*b-4*a*c))/(2*a);
    root12= (-b + sqrt(b*b-4*a*c))/(2*a);
    printf ("root 1 = &f, root 2 = %f\n", root1, root2);
}
else {
    printf ("It is not quadratic equation\n");
}
```

Practice

- Expand program to find the roots of various quadratic equations (various combination of the coefficients) and find the roots of given quadratic equations.
- $x^2 - 3x + 1 = 0$
- $x + 1 = 0$
- $x^2 + x + 1 = 0$
- $x^2 + 2x + 1 = 0$

KeyPoints

+ (D < 0)

- The value of D is less than 0

Output

GUESS??

1) What is the difference between the project to solve quadratic equation and Project 04 to solve quadratic equation?

2) If we represent `(2 * a)` to `2 * a` without brackets like `(-b + sqrt(b * b - 4 * a * c)) / 2 * a`, is it same with the previous one? Why are the roots formula different? What is the meaning of `(-b + sqrt(b * b - 4 * a * c)) / 2 / a`?

3) If we represent `(2 * a)` to `(2a)` like `(-b + sqrt(b * b - 4 * a * c)) / (2a)`, is it same with the previous one? Let's execute!! What is the reason for this output?

4) Can we calculate other mathematical functions such as sin, cos, exp, log, a^b, etc. besides the square root? Which function should be used?

Project 06

The Coding Strategy for Troubleshooting

Finding Simple Number Game

Project Description

Perform the following tasks based on the number inputted with the keyboard

- If the number is less than 1 or greater than 9, output "Please input between 1~8" message
- If the number is 2, output "Congratulation" message
- If the number is neither of them, output "Sorry" message

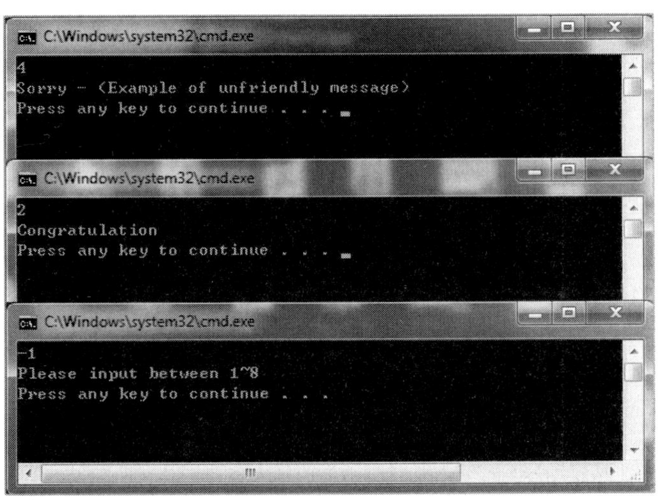

Main Concepts

Message

String that provides information to program user

Comparison Operation

Logic Operation

- Represent comparison operation using relational operator such as over, under, greater than, less than, same, different and etc.

  `>` `<` `>=` `<=` `==` `!=`

  Ref. 'Same' uses `==`

- Represent logic operation (AND, OR, NOT) using logical operators below

  `&&` `||` `!`

  Ref. `&` and `|` is not one unit, but two units like `&&` and `||`

Main Objectives

- Input the value through keyboard using `scanf()`
- Value comparison representation
- Decide `true` and `false`
- Utilize `if` statement

06.01 Creating and executing project

⑨ Input the value through keyboard

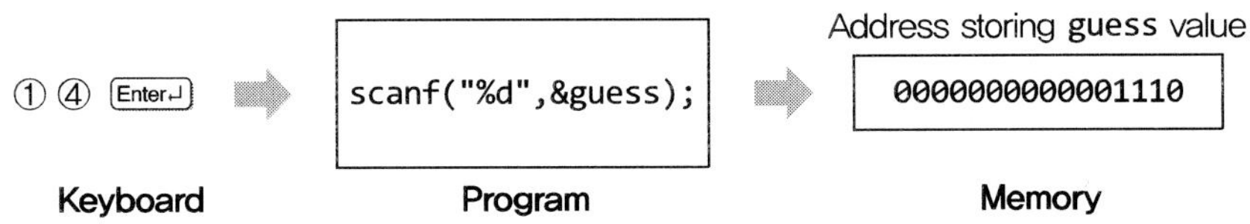

Practice

Creating and executing project

✻ Project creation and completion

- After project creation, add main.cpp as new item and code main.cpp

✻ Test given cases

- 0
- 9
- 2

✻ Try the cases below to check the usage of scanf()

- Edit &guess to guess and execute
- Edit %d to d without % and execute
- Edit %d to %f or %e and execute
- Edit %d to %3d or %5d and execute

Ref.

In Visual Studio 2013, #define is required to use scanf()

```
#define _CRT_SECURE_NO_WARNINGS
```

KeyPoints

+ scanf format

- Integer uses %d
- %5d outputs the value to 5 digits
- %10d outputs the value to 10 digits
- & is essential in front of variable

Output

06.02 Generating and applying random number

Procedure for generating random number

Step 1 Header file **#include**

```
#include <stdlib.h>
#include <time.h>
```

Step 2 Call **srand((unsigned int)time(NULL));**

Step 3 Call **rand()** and then return generated random number

– If you need a random integer between 0~7, take the remaining after **rand()** is divided by 8

– `rand() % 8`

Practice

＊ Method of dynamically assigning the game's `target` value by generating random number

＊ Edit program and execute

- Edit the program to use random number on the basis of above procedures for generating random number
  - Edit `target=2;`
  - To `target = rand() % 8 + 1;`
- After executing the program, input 2
- After executing again, input 3

KeyPoints

+ % operator

- Calculate remainder
- The result of 10 % 3 is 1

Output

Practice

* Understand random number generating program through following cases
  - After editing `#include <stdlib.h>` to comment, execute
  - After editing `srand((unsigned int)time());` to `srand(1);`, execute many times

* Review debugger
  - Set a break point to `target = rand( ) % 8 + 1;`
  - Execute debugger mode (Use F5 key or menu)
  - While proceeding debugging using F10, check target value
    - Wait for a moment after putting the mouse pointer over variables
    - Or add `target` to investigation window

KeyPoints

+ **time()**
  - Function to find computer internal time

Output

06.03 Creating friendly program

Reinforce response regarding input

Output friendly message at all times

- If input is correct ⇒ Output `"Congratulation\n"`
- If input is greater than **target** ⇒ Output `"Greater than target\n"`
- If input is less than **target** ⇒ Output `"Less than target\n"`
  - ⇨ Program should select different behaviors based on diverse conditions

```
if (guess) == target)    {   }
else if (guess < target) {   }
else                     {   }
```

Practice

Edit and execute code to output message even if the answer is incorrect

＊ Edit program

```
▸ if (guess == target)       Output "Congratulation"
  else if (target < guess)   Output "Greater than Target"
  else                       Output "Less than Target"
```

KeyPoints

+ Comparison Operator

- Same : ==
- Over : >
- Under : <
- Different : !=
- Less than : <=
- Greater than : >=

Output

Practice

✻ Review comparison operators

- Edit `if (guess==target)` to `if (guess = target)` and execute

✻ Find the input order that can guess the `target` value within 4 times. The `target` value is between 1 ~ 8

- When `target = 3`
- When `target = 8`
- When `target = 2`

✻ At most, how many times does it take to guess the `target` value if the `target` is greater than 1 and less than 15?

Output

GUESS??

1) How are the logic value `true` and `false` are represented in C language? is 2 or 3 `true`? are non-zero values `true`?

2) What is the value of given logical expressions?

   (1) `(1 == 2)`

   (2) `(1 > 2)`

   (3) `(1 == 2) && ( 1 > 2)`

   (4) `(1 = 2)  && ( 1 < 2)`

3) What is the expected output of given commands?

```
if (1)
     printf("true\n");
else
     printf("false\n");
```

4) What is the expected output of given commands?

```
if ( a = b)
    printf(" a = b \n");
else
    printf(" a != b \n");
```

5) What are some useful examples of random number in the real world?

Project 07

The Coding Strategy for Troubleshooting

Finding Randomly Created Number Game

Project Description

Write a game program that guesses hidden number between 1 to 8.

- Set randomly integer between 1 to 8
- Terminate program if input is under 1 or greater than 9
- If correct, output "Congratulation" and terminate program
- If neither of above cases, output appropriate message and continue progress

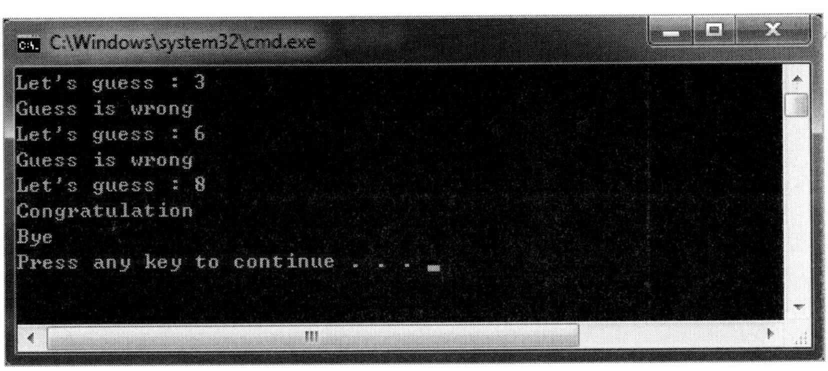

Main Concepts

Random number

For the generated numbers to become random numbers two conditions must be fulfilled

- The generated numbers should be uniformly distributed
- It should not be able to estimate the next number using previous numbers

Loop(iteration, repetition) statement

If the condition is `true`, exit loop with `break` command

```
while (1) {
    . . .
    if (Condition) break;
    . . .
}
```

Main Objectives

- ✎ Extract iterative behavior from problem
- ✎ Code extracted iterative behavior
- ✎ Exit command of iterative behavior(`break`)
- ✎ Simplify coding by using `#define`

07.01 Coding iterative behavior

⑥ Coding iterative behavior

(Requirements) "If it is not above two cases, ... continue progress"

⇨

Continue game until user guesses correct number or request termination	Decision	Accept input value
		Exit iterative behavior if there is request for termination
	Operation	When user guesses correct number, output appropriate message and exit loop
		When user guesses wrong number, output appropriate message and continue loop

⇨
```
while(1) {
    Accept input value;
    if (Request for termination) break;
    if (Correct) Output message and exit loop;
    Depending on situations, output appropriate message;
}
```

Practice

Project creation and execution

* Project creation and coding
  - After project creation, add main.cpp as new item
  - Code main.cpp
    - Coding main.cpp by referring and extending `main()` function of Project 06

Output

Practice

✻ Execution

- Input 0 or 9
- Input the value to correctly guess generated random number less than 4 times

✻ Meaning of break; command

- Add `break;` below `scanf("%d", &guess);` and execute

✻ Execution of `while( )` statement

- Edit `while(1)` to `while(0)` and execute
- Edit `while(1)` to `while(2)` and execute
- Edit `while(1)` to `while(true)` and execute
- Edit `while(1)` to `while(false)` and execute

KeyPoints

+ break;

- Exit while loop statement

+ while(Condition) { }

- If condition is true, enter body (iterative command)
- If condition is false, terminate while and execute next command

+ 0 is false, the other is true

Output

07.02 Understand iterative execution and extending target

◎ Coding easily editable program using **#define**

- `#define UPPERBOUND  15`

  Using given command, define target range to be guessed

  ⇨ When editing target range, only the **#define** command has to be edited If we use numbers directly in code, it is required to edit every line

- `#define HELP " ... "`

  Define output message using **#define**

Practice

＊ Edit code to use #define (Refer to code below)

▸
```
#define UPPERBOUND  15
target = rand() % UPPERBOUND + 1;
if((guess < 1) || (guess > UPPERBOUND) break;
```

▸
```
#define HELP " ... "
printf(HELP);      // Different with printf("HELP");
```

KeyPoints

+ Good program
- Readable
- Editable
- Efficient and reliable program

Output

Practice

※ Execution

- Input 0 or 16
- Input 5
- Input to correctly guess generated random number within 4 times

※ Observe iterative behavior using debugger

- Set break point to `while(1)` and execute debugger with F5
- Add `guess` and `target` to investigation window
- Observe executed command whenever F10 is pushed
  Whenever you encounter `scanf()`, input value to proceed to next command
- Input 0 to observe termination of loop statement

Output

07.03 Extending program feature

Practice

Requirements

1) Output the number of tries at the end of execution
2) Accept input UPPERBOUND from user and apply

* Edit Program

- Add new variable for the number of try

```
int trial = 0;
trial++;
printf("Number of tries : %d\n", trial);
```

- Make UPPERBOUND as variable

```
//#define MSGUPPERBOUND " ... "
#define   MAXUP   128
int UPPERBOUND = 8 ;
printf(MSGUPPERBOUND);
scanf("%d", &UPPERBOUND);
if (UPPERBOUND <= 1 || UPPERBOUND > MAXUP) {
    printf(MSGERRUP);
    return 0;
}
```

* Execution

- Input diverse number as UPPERBOUND value and execute game
  0, 1, 9, 80, 255

KeyPoints

+ Variable declaration and initialization
- It is good to declare and initialize variable at the same time
- It is called default value

+ Way to increase reliability
- Proceed program after verifying input data

Output

GUESS??

1) What is the iterative behaviors in the given situations and when it is terminated?

   (1) Walking to take the bus after school

   (2) Sum of two three digit numbers (e.g. 123 + 987)

   (3) Multiplication between two digit numbers (e.g. 34 * 42)

2) There is no code that does not use loop statement. What is the reason for that?

3) When you execute the given code, how many time are "here₩n" output?

(1)

```
while(1) ; {          // be careful ; in front of {
    printf("here\n");
}
```

(2)

```
while(1)  {
    printf("here\n");
}
```

Project 08

The Coding Strategy for Troubleshooting

Finding GCD and LCM

Project Description

Find the GCD and LCM of two natural numbers inputted by keyboard Following is the expected output.

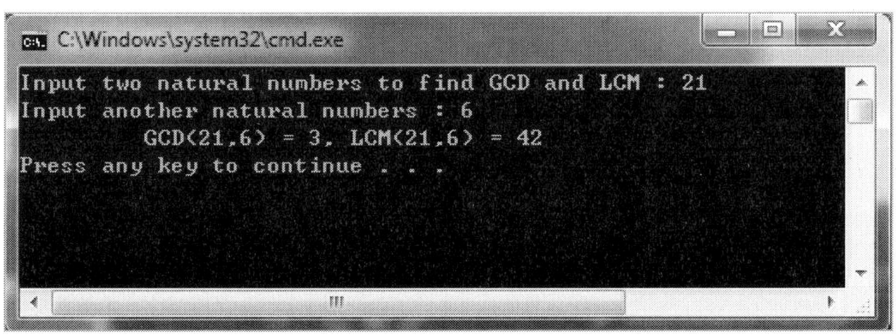

Main Concepts

Greatest Common Divisor

- GCD(Greatest Common Divisor)
  Greatest value among common divisors of two numbers

- Euclid(Greek mathematician) Method
  GCD(a, b) = GCD(b, a % b), a or b is non-zero

  If b is 0, a is GCD(a, b)
  GCD(6, 21) = GCD(21, 6) = GCD(6, 3) = GCD(3, 0) = 3

Least Common Multiple

- LCM(Least Common Multiple)
  Least value among common multiples of two numbers

- Formula to find LCM using GCD
  LCM(a, b) = |a * b| / GCD(a, b)

Main Objectives

- ✎ Compose program with two or more source files
- ✎ Review the loop statement
- ✎ Need of data verification
- ✎ Modulo operation (%)

08.01 Abstraction and **main()** partition

◎ Program structuralization and abstraction

Main work flow of program

- Input two natural numbers
- Find GCD ⇒ Because we will make this as function, just call this function in **main()**
- Find LCM
- Output calculated GCD and LCM

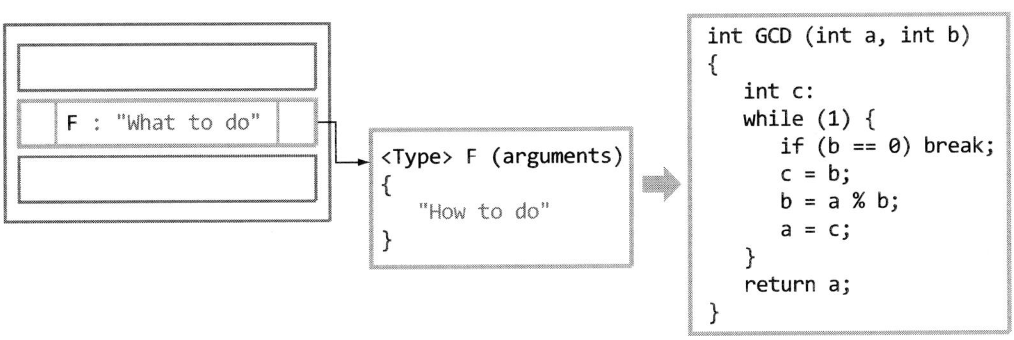

Practice

Create project composing of 3 files and execute

* Project creation and coding
  - After project creation, copy gcd.cpp and gcd.h to project folder
  - Add gcd.cpp and gcd.h as existing item
  - Add main.cpp as new item and code

* Calculate GCD and LCM of given pairs
  - 6, 16
  - 0, 32
  - -24, 42
  - -24, -42

* Trace GCD calculation process using debugger
  - Set break point to `while(1)` of function `GCD()`
  - Execute debugger with F5
  - Reach break point after input 6 and 16
  - After reaching break point, trace the value of variable while progressing with F10

KeyPoints

+ break;
- Exit while loop

+ % operator
- Calculate the remainder
- Value of 7%2 is 1

+ #include header file
- When we use the function defined in a different file, we add header file
- Whenever .cpp file is created, create a matching .h header file

Output

08.02 Understand modulo (%) operator

⑨ Test % operator calculating the remainder

```
#define _CRT_SECURE_NO_WARNINGS
#include <stdio.h>
int main(void)
{
    int  k, m;
    while (1) {
       printf("Enter two integers (-9 –9 to terminate) : ");
       scanf("%d %d", &k, &m);
       if (k == -9 && m == -9) break;
       printf("\t %d modulo %d = %d \n", k, m, k % m);
    }
    return 0;
}
```

Practice

Complete project for testing % operator and execute

* Execute given test cases one by one
  - 10 2
  - 10 3
  - 10 -3
  - 0 4
  - -9 -9

KeyPoints

+ **scanf**
("%d %d", &k, &m)
Input two number at the same time
(e.g.) 10 3

+ **%**
It does not point out the remainder of the strict meaning
(e.g.) -10 % 3 == -1

Output

08.03 Implement requirements precisely

Practice

Implementing requirements below and testing

Requirements

Calculate GCD and LCM of two natural numbers

✻ Edit main() function

- If input number is negative, it is converted to positive(natural number) and used

```
#include <math.h>
a = abs(a);
```

- If at least one input value is 0, output appropriate error message

```
if (a * b == 0) {
    printf(ERRMSG);
    return 0;
}
```

✻ Execute given test cases

- 6, 16
- 0, 32
- -24, 42
- -24, -42

✻ Header file test

- Edit #include "gcd.h" to comment and execute
- Edit to #include <gcd.h> and execute

KeyPoints

+ abs() of <math.h>

- Function to find absolute value

+ Requirement

- Function or condition that program should handle
- Understanding the requirements are the most important thing to make a proper program

+ Header File "" and <>

- <> : System provide
- "" : My project

Output

GUESS??

1) Is there a point to do modulo operation (%, operation to calculate the remainder) on real numbers? For example, what is the result of 21.5 % 6?

2) What is the result of −22% 6? How can we get the remainder of dividing a negative number with a positive number? What is the definition of the remainder?

3) What happened in the Korean peninsula around 300 BC when Euclid was alive?
Appreciate the time when the following historical figures were around.

(1) Alexander the Great(356 ~ 323 BC)
(2) Silla(新羅, 57 BC ~ 935 AD)
(3) Confucius(孔子, 551 ~ 479 BC)
(4) Solomon(1037 ~ 998 BC)

Project 09

Decimal to Binary

Project Description

Write a program that converts the number inputted by keyboard from decimal to binary and outputs the following window.

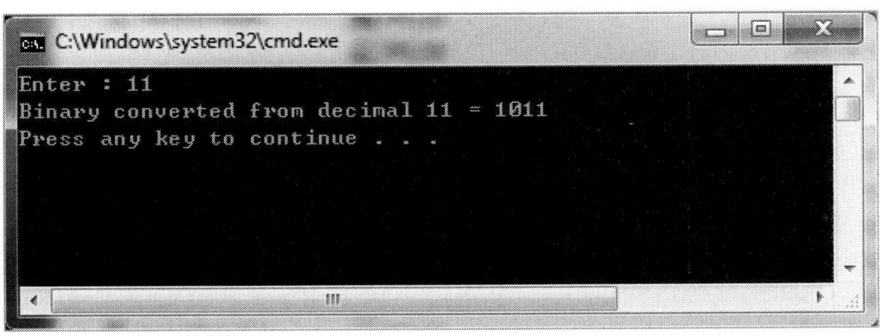

Main Concepts

Numeral system

- **r−numeral system number** $a_n a_{n-1} \cdots a_1 a_0$ is
  - r-numeral system number is represented as $a_n r^n + a_{n-1} r^{n-1} + \cdots a_1 r^1 + a_0$

– Binary number 1011 in decimal number is $1 * 2^3 + 0 * 2^2 + 1 * 2^1 + 1 = 11$

- Method of converting decimal number to binary number
  - ✓ $11 = a_n 2^n + \cdots + a_1 2^1 + a_0 2^0$

    Calculate the remainder. Divide both sides by 2. The remainder of left side is 1, that of right side $a_0 = 1$
  - ✓ $5 = a_n 2^{n-1} + \cdots + a_1$

    Calculate the remainder. Divide both sides by 2. The remainder of left side is 1, that of right side $a_1 = 1$
  - ✓ $2 = a_n 2^{n-2} + \cdots + a_2$

    Calculate the remainder. Divide both sides by 2. The remainder of left side is 1, that of right side $a_2 = 0$
  - ✓ $1 = a_n 2^{n-3} + \cdots + a_3$

    Calculate the remainder. Divide both sides by 2. The remainder of left side is 1, that of right side $a_3 = 1$
  - ✓ When the left side become 0, the conversion process ends binary number is 1011

Main Objectives

- ✎ Compose program with two or more source files
- ✎ Review the loop statement
- ✎ Need of data verification
- ✎ Modulo operation (%)

09.01 Abstraction and **main()** partition

Program structuralization and abstraction

Main work flow of program

- Input decimal number
- Convert to binary number ⇒ Because we will make this as function, just call this function in **main()**

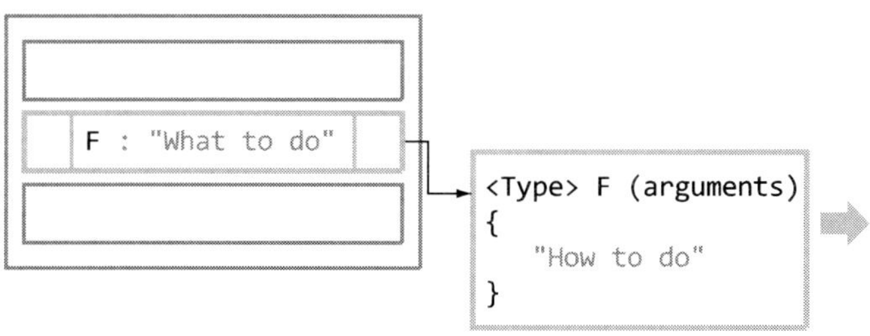


```
int Dec2Bin(int dec)
{
   int rem, tmp, bin;
   tmp = 1;
   bin = 0;
   while (1) {
      if (dec == 0) break;
      rem = dec % 2;
      dec = dec / 2;
      bin = bin + rem * tmp;
      tmp = tmp * 10;
   }
   return bin;
}
```

- Output converted binary number

Practice

Create project composing of 3 file and execute

✻ Project completion

- Project creation
- Copy dec2bin.cpp and dec2bin.h to project folder
- Add dec2bin.cpp and dec2bin.h as new item
- Add main.cpp as new item and code

✻ Test various decimal number

- 2
- 7
- 11
- 65535 (2^{16}-1)
- -9

Output

KeyPoints

+ Dec2Bin()

- Function to convert decimal to binary
- Return converted binary number

+ Representation of 0~15 as binary

0000, 0001, 0010, 0011, 0100, 0101, 0110, 0111, 1000, 1001, 1010, 1011, 1100, 1101, 1110, 1111

+ If the number of 1 is N, 2^N-1

- Summation of N-ary geometric series with first term 1 and common ratio 2

09.02 Analyze the limitation of data representation

Represent integer with n-bit

- The representation range of `int`(Representing two's complement)
  - Positive number : 000...000 ~ 011...111 that is, $0 \sim 2^{n-1} - 1$
  - Negative number : 111...111 ~ 100...000 that is, $-1 \sim -2^{n-1}$
  - In case of n = 16,
    $-2^{15} \sim 2^{15}-1$, that is -65536 ~ 65535
  - In case of n = 32,
    $-2^{31} \sim 2^{31}-1$, that is -2,147,483,648 ~ 2,147,483,647(About 2 billion, 10 digits)
- The representation range of `unsigned int`
  - $0 \sim 2^{32} - 1$, that is 0 ~ 4,294,967,295(About 4 billion)

Practice

※ Convert given decimal to binary

- 1023 (Ref. $2^{10} - 1$, that is 1,111,111,111)
- 1024 (Ref. 2^{10}, that is 10,000,000,000)
- 2047 (Ref. $2^{11} - 1$, that is 11,111,111,111)

※ Check the cause of errors by analyzing `Dec2Bin()` through debugger

- After setting `while(1)` of `Dec2Bin()` as break point, execute debugger with F5
- After inputting 2047 and reaching break point, add `dec` and `bin` to investigation window
- Trace converting process while proceeding step by step with F10

※ Edit program to convert only decimal between 0~1023 to binary

- Accept input value with `scanf()`, and if the vinput value is beyond processing range output error

```
if (dec < 0 || dec > 1023) {
    printf("Beyond the processing range\n");
    return 0;
}
```

KeyPoints

+ sizeof(<type>)

- The number of used bit to represent data of <type>

(e.g.)

```
sizeof(int)
sizeof(float)
sizeof(char)
```

Output

GUESS??

1) What is binary number of 4, 8, 16, 32, etc.?

2) What is binary number of 1024?

3) How far can you count with your fingers? 10, 20, or 128? How far can you count if you also use your toes?

4) In case of r–numeral system, $a_n\ a_{n-1} \cdots\ a_1\ a_0$ should be represented only using 0, 1, 2, ⋯ , r–1. Hexadecimal only use 0, 1, 2, ⋯, 9, A, B, C, D, E, F. In this time, A of hexadecimal converts 10 of decimal number, and B=11, C=12, D=13, E=14, F=15. Represent decimal number 28 in hexadecimal. What is decimal number of hexadecimal 0F?

5) In computer engineering, binary, octal, decimal and hexadecimal are popular. The way to convert binary to octal is dividing 3–bit in binary and converting. Why is that? How many bits should be divided in binary to convert hexadecimal? If there are 16–bits, how many ways can it be expressed in hexadecimal?

Project **10** The Coding Strategy for Troubleshooting

Binary to Decimal

Project Description

Write a program that converts the number inputted by keyboard from binary to decimal and outputs the following window.

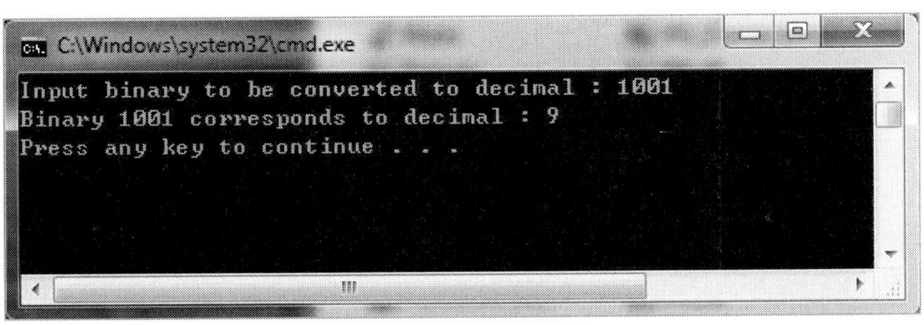

Main Concepts

Numeral systems

- The way to convert binary number $A = a_n a_{n-1} \cdots a_1 a_0$ to decimal number
  - ✓ $S = 0$
  - ✓ $a_0 = A \% 10$, $A = A / 10$, $S = S + a_0*2^0$
  - ✓ $a_1 = A \% 10$, $A = A / 10$, $S = S + a_1*2^1$
  - ✓ $a_2 = A \% 10$, $A = A / 10$, $S = S + a_2*2^2$
  - ✓ . . .
  - ✓ $a_n = A \% 10$, $A = A / 10$, $S = S + a_n*2^n$
  - ✓ If $A = 0$, terminate converting process

Main Objectives

- ✎ Compose program with two or more source files
- ✎ Review the loop statement
- ✎ Need of data verification
- ✎ Modulo operation (%), Integer division, `pow()` function

10.01 Abstraction and **main()** partition

◎ Program structuralization and abstraction

Main work flow of program

- Input binary number
- Convert to decimal number ⇒ Because we will make this as function, just call this function in **main()**
- Output converted decimal number

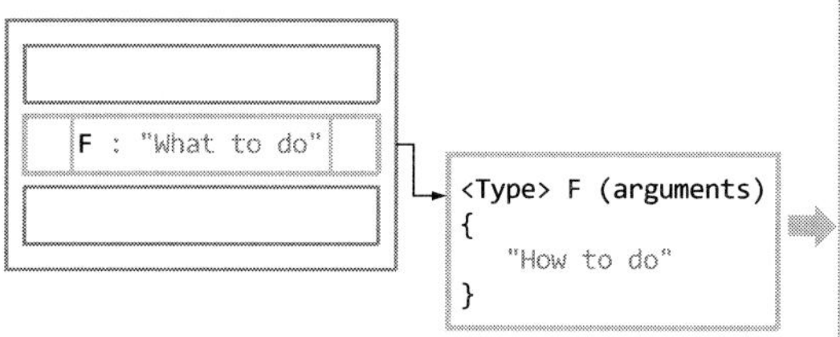


```
#include <math.h>
int Bin2Dec(int  bin)    /* Find bug in following program. */
{
   int dec, tmp, rem;
   tmp=0;
   while (1) (
      if (bin == 0) break;
      rem = bin % 10;
      bin = bin / 10;
      dec = dec+rem*pow(2,tmp);
      tem = tmp + 1; /*pow(2,n) = n—square of 2*/
   }
   return dec;
}
```

Practice

Create project composing of 3 file and execute

※ Project completion

- Project creation
- Copy bin2dec.cpp and bin2dec.h to project folder
- Add bin2dec.cpp and bin2dec.h as new item
- Add main.cpp as new item and write a code

※ Test various binary number (',' should be omitted in input)

- 1,001
- 1,111,111 (The number of 1 is 7)
- 10,000,000,000 (The number of 1 is 1 and 0 is 10)
- 11,111,111,111 (The number of 1 is 11)
- -1,000
- 1,002 (Not binary)

KeyPoints

+ Bin2Dec()

- Function to convert binary to decimal
- Return converted decimal number

+ The range of 32-bit integer

- Summation of N-ary geometric series with first term 1 and common ratio 2
- About -2 billion ~ 2 billion

+ Binary number

- Represented by only 0 or 1

Output

10.02 Analyze conversion program

pow(x,y)

Analyze the problem

- Current `Bin2Dec()` code uses `pow(2.0, tmp)`
- During the processing of `while` loop, 2^0, 2^1, 2^2, 2^3, ... 2^n are calculated using `pow()` one by one

```
tmp = 0;
while (1) {
    ...
    dec = dec + rem*pow(2.0, tmp); /*pow(2, n)= N-square of 2*/
    tmp = tmp + 1;
}
```

`pow(x, y)` is a function that takes a while to calculate

Solution

- 2^0, 2^1, 2^2, 2^3, ... 2^n can be calculated using simple multiplications
  - If `pow2n = 1` is initial value, calculate `pow2n = pow2n*2` each time,
  - Sequentially 2^0, 2^1, 2^2, 2^3, ... , 2^n are calculated

```
int pow2n = 1;
while (1) {
    . . .
    dec = dec + rem*pow2n; /*Sequentially 2^0, 2^1, 2^2, 2^3 are calculated */
    pow2n= pow2n* 2;
}
```

Practice

* Edit program to not use `pow()` function and execute
  - Input 1001
  - Input 1111

* Analyze converting process using debugger
  - Set break point to `while(1)` of `Bin2Dec()`
  - After executing debugger with F5, input 1001 and reach to break point
  - Check pow2n value while proceeding each command with F10
    - Check whether 2^0, 2^1, 2^2, 2^3 are correctly calculated one by one

KeyPoints

+ pow(x, y)

Calculates x^y

#include <math.h>

Output

10.03 Verifying input data

Verification of input data

- Is it binary number?
  - Binary number is represented by only 0 and 1
- Is the value in the convertible range?
  - Inform user about convertible range
  - If the input is beyond the range, handle as error

Practice

✻ Check binary number notation

- Ref. rem calculated by rem = bin%10; is 0 or 1
- Edit Bin2Dec()

```
if (rem > 1 || rem < 0)
    Because it is error, stop converting and return 0
```

- Execute and input 1002

✻ Output how to use program and verify input data

```
#define HELP ". . . Please input value in range : "
printf(HELP); scanf("%d", &bin);
if (bin < ALLOWEDMIN || bin > ALLOWEDMAX) {
    Handle as error
}
```

KeyPoints

+ Binary
- Use only 0 and 1

+ rem=bin%10
- If bin is binary, rem should be 0 or 1
- If rem is not 0 or 1, bin is not binary

Output

GUESS??

1) Represent general term a_n of series 1, 2^1, 2^2, 2^3, ... in recurrence formula.

2) Compare performance between calculating 2^1, 2^2, ... , 2^{10} using **pow(2.0, n)**, n =0, 1, 2, ..., 10 and calculating 2^1, 2^2, ... , 2^{10} using simple multiplication.

[Performance comparison method]

```
time1 = stop watch start;
   calculate 2^1, 2^2, ... , 2^10 with 10,000 times pow()
time2 = stop watch stop;
time3 = stop watch start;
   calculate 2^1, 2^2, ... , 2^10 with 10,000 times multiplication
time4 = stop watch stop;
Compare time2-time1 and time4-time3
```

3) r–numeral system only uses the number(or symbol) among 0, 1, 2, ... , r–1. Can we verify whether the input value is appropriate for r–numeral system notation? For reference, hexadecimal uses up to A, B, C, D, E, F.

Project 11

The Coding Strategy for Troubleshooting

Solving f(x) = 0

Project Description

Write a program that finds an approximate root of $f(x) = 3x - 1 = 0$ which is a continuous function within the interval of [v, w]. Use bisection method to calculate the root. If there is no approximate root for $y = f(x)$ within the given interval (ex: sign of f(v) and f(w) are same), then exit the program after displaying request for inputting a valid interval values of v and w.

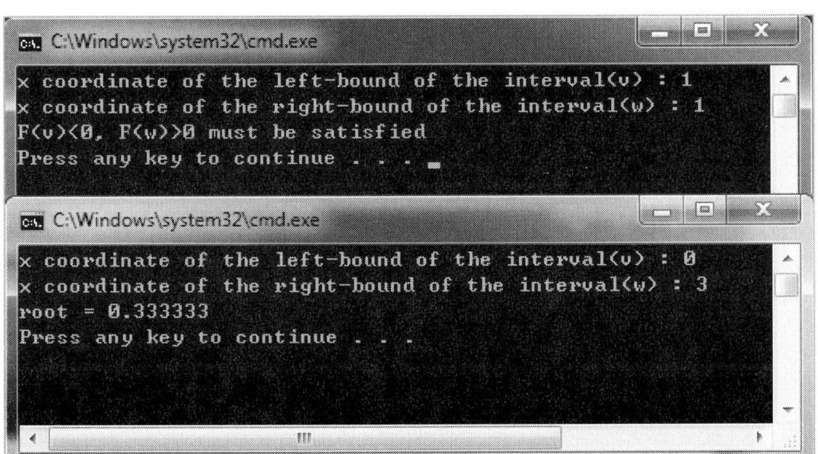

Main Concepts

bisection

- If y = f(x) is the continuous function withing the closed interval of [v, w] and f(v) * f(w) < 0, then f(x) = 0 must have at least one root in the open interval (v, w).
- The process is continued until the interval is sufficiently small for the root.

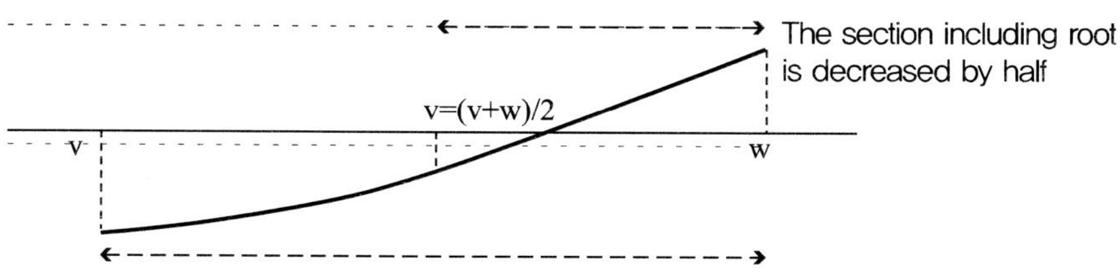

Main Objectives

- Modeling of repeated calculation
- Exit condition of repeated task
- `double` and `float`
- Using `#define`

11.01 Repeated task implementation

Repeated Task Modeling (f(v) < 0, f(w) > 0 case)

<table>
<tr><td rowspan="5">Repeat until the interval is sufficiently small or a root is found</td><td rowspan="2">decision</td><td colspan="2">stop repetition when the interval is sufficiently small</td></tr>
<tr><td colspan="2">calculate the root of f(mid), where mid = (v + w) / 2</td></tr>
<tr><td rowspan="3">task</td><td rowspan="3">test for mid is root, if not adjust the interval</td><td>(f(mid) == 0) → mid is the root</td></tr>
<tr><td>(f(mid) < 0) → new interval [mid, w]</td></tr>
<tr><td>(f(mid) > 0) → new interval [v, mid]</td></tr>
</table>

```
int main(void)
{
    float  v, w, mid, fmid;

    printf(PROMPT4V);
    scanf("%f",&v);
    printf(PROMPT4W);
    scanf("%f",&w);

    // validate input data
    while(1)  {
        if ((w-v) <= EPSILON) break;
        // repeat task command
    }
    printf("root = %f\n",(v+w)/2);

    return 0;
}
```

Practice

※ Project completion and execution

- Project creation
- New item main.cpp creation and coding
- Execute test cases below
  - when interval is [0, 2]
  - when interval is [-1, 1]
  - when interval is [1, 2]

Output

11.02 Structuring program

Structure of main()

Problem

`main()` defines all the codes

Solution

Code after defining functions that have independent functionality

- separation of bisection functionality

  Code just bisection part

  - `float bisection(float v, float w, float *root);`
  - If root is found, save the **root** and **return** 0, otherwise **return** -1

- Define the function that finds the root separately
  - macro

    ```
    #define F(x)  (3*(x) - 1)
    ```

  - or define as a function

    ```
    float F(float x)  { return 3*x -1; }
    ```

Practice

Convert the given `main()` to all comments and write a new `main()`

* Replace the logic that calculate the root in `main()` with the function call
  - `ret = bisection(v, w, &root); //need & in front of root`

* Place the code of `bisection()` function above `main()` function

```
int bisection (float v, float w, float *root)
{
    float mid, fmid;
    if (!(F(v) < 0) && (F(w) > 0)) return -1;
     //-----------------------------------//
     //  Implement bisection algorithm      //
     //-----------------------------------//
     *root = (v+w)/2;  // save root. Cautious about usage of *
     return 0;
}
```

* Implement `F(x)` as a macro or a function and place it above the `bisection()` function code

* Execute program

KeyPoints

+ Parameter passing method

- & is used in the calling function
- &root refers to the address of where the value of root is saved
- In the called function, * is used. *root=(v+w)/2;
- *root dereferences the address of root. Therefore, save the value, (v+w)/2, to the address of root. (ref) input value of a scanf("%d",&a);

Output

11.03 Modifying bisection()

◎ Generalize the function by removing the dependency of data

(1) need to handle $F(v) > 0$, $F(w) < 0$ cases

(2) Forcefully stop the infinite repetition

- Need to increase the repeated number by 1 everytime it repeats and forcefully stop the repetition when the repeated number reaches to a threshold value

Practice

※ Modify F(x) to find the root of -3x + 1 = 0 and find the root of F(x) in the interval of [0, 3]

▸ `#define F(x) (-3*(x) + 1)`

※ Modify F(x) so it can handle F(v) > 0, F(w) < 0 cases

▸ call bisection() by exchanging v and w

```
if (F(v) < 0 && F(w) > 0)
     ret = bisection(v, w, &root);
else if (F(v) > 0 && F(w) < 0)
     ret = bisection(w, v, &root);
else
     error;
```

Ref. bisection() does not assume either v is first parameter nor w is second parameter

Output

Practice

※ Modify bisection() so that it repeats up to the maximun number.

- Modify bisection()

  int bisection(float v, float w, int max, float *root); add

  int cnt = 0; add

  while(1) { } add the below code inside the while loop

  ```
  cnt++;
  if (cnt > max) return -1;
  ```

- Modify main()

  ret = bisection(v, w, 30, &root); add the maximum repetition

Output

GUESS??

1) Find the function that has root in the interval of [v, w] and f(v) * f(w) 〉 0.

2) The interval is reduced in half with one bisection. Guess how many repetition is needed if we want to reduce the interval less the 10^{-6}.

3) What do you think that it is the most valuable benefit to use bisection?

4) What about the drawbacks using bisection? How can you use the bisection if you do not know the interval of the function for the existing root?

5) What does `*root = (v+w)/2;` mean to you in the function `bisection()`?

Project 12

The Coding Strategy for Troubleshooting

Solving Fibonacci Rabbit Problem

Project Description

In his book *Liber Abaci*, Italian Mathematician Leonardo of Pisa (1170-1250) posed this question

Suppose a newly-born pair of rabbits, one male, one female, are put in a field. Rabbits are able to mate at the age of one month so that at the end of its second month a female can produce another pair of rabbits. Suppose that our rabbits never die and that the female always produces one new pair (one male, one female) every month from the second month on. How many pairs will there be in one year?

Write a program that calculates the number of pairs after n months.

Ref. Leonard of Pisa is also known as Fibonacci.

Main Concepts

Recurrence relation

- The number of pair of rabbits for the first 11 months are

  1, 1, 2, 3, 5, 8, 13, 21, 34, 55, 89, 144, . .

- The first two 1s are the number of pairs for the first and second month. Therefore, the Fibonacci sequence starts with two 1s (1,1,). If you draw a graph it would be more clear

- The first pair conceives a pair of rabits after 1 month, and gives birth on the second month.

- When F_n indicates the pairs of rabbits on the nth month, the following recurrence relation establishes.

  $F_n = F_{n-1} + F_{n-2}$, n = 2, 3, ...

  $F_0 = 1,\ F_1 = 1$

- The relation between the general term (F_n, F_{n-1}, ...) is called recurrence relation

Main Objectives

✎ Using recurrence relation modeling for repetitive tasks

✎ Recurrence relations coding

12.01 Simple recurrence relation programing

Testing Program

- The following equation shows the sum of 1 to n

S_n = n_{th} sum,

$S_0 = 0$, $S_n = S_{n-1} + n$

- Pseudo code of recurrence relation

```
S = 0;
for k = 1, 2, 3, 4, ... , n
    S = S + k;   // i.e., if k = 1 the value of S is equal to S + 1
```

- Converting the pseudo code to C

```
S = 0;
for (k=1; k<=n; k++)
    S = S + k;  // or S += k;
```

Practice

Using the method above, code the following problems

✻ The sum of 1 to n

✻ n! = 1 * 2 * 3 * ... * n

▸ (Recurrence relation) $f_n = f_{n-1} * n$, $f_1 = 1$

✻ $a^n = a * a * ... * a$ (n multiplication)

▸ (Recurrence relation) $p_n = p_{n-1} * a$, $p_0 = 1$

✻ $a_1 = 1$, when the common difference is d(constant) nth of the arithmetic sequence

▸ (Recurrence relation) $a_n = a_{n-1} + d$, $a_1 = 1$

✻ $t_n = a^n / n!$, $t_0 = 1$, a is constant

▸ (Recurrence relation) $t_n = t_{n-1} * a / n$, $t_0 = 1$

KeyPoints

+ **meaning of for statement**
  - for k=1,2,3,..,n for(k=1;k<=n;k++)
  - for m=2,4,6,..,20 for(m=2;m<=20;m+=2)

+ **x+=exp;**

  x=x+(exp);meaing (caution)

+ **x-=exp;**

  The meaning of x=x-(exp); is different from x=x-exp; think of x-=2-3;

Output

12.02 Fibonacci recurrence relation coding

⑨ Implementing the recurrence relation of the Fibonacci sequence with iteration

- Recurrence Relation

  $F_n = F_{n-1} + F_{n-2}$, $n = 2, 3, \ldots$, $F_0 = 1$, $F_1 = 1$

- It can be expressed with 2 variables (combination of 2 previous terms)

```
Fn1 = 1; Fn = 1; //When n = 1, define these two to figure out the following
When n=2, tmp = Fn; Fn = Fn + Fn1; Fn1 = tmp;
When n=3, tmp = Fn; Fn = Fn + Fn1; Fn1 = tmp;
. . .
```

- Coding result

```
Fn1 = 1; Fn = 1;
for (k = 2; k <= n; k++) {
    tmp = Fn;
    Fn = Fn + Fn1;
    Fn1 =  tmp;
}
```

Practice

Run after project completion

* Calculate the number of pairs of rabbits by using 12 months or 2 years for the value of n

* Gather the output of Fn/Fn-1 and check if it gradually reaches 1.618 (1.618 is considered to be the golden ratio)

```
ratio = Fn/Fn1;
printf("ratio(%3d) = %.3f\n", k, ratio);
```

KeyPoints

- **φ : golden ratio**
  $\varphi = (a+b)/a = a/b$
  $1 + \varphi = 1/\varphi$
  root of quadratic equation
- **There are a lot of nature and famous sculptures that follow the golden ratio**

Output

12.03 Implementing after expressing with Recurrence Relation

◎ Recurrence Relations Modeling

Steps

- Check if the problem requires repetitive statement
- Indicate repetitive unit behavior with general term of recurrence relation
- Indicate the relation between F_n and the previous result F_{n-1}

Application

$f(x) = 0$, $a < x < b$, Review of bisection on calculating the root

- Calculate the interval where the root exists
- Suppose $I_n = (a_n, b_n)$, $a_0 = a$, $b_0 = b$
- Calculate I_n from I_{n-1}

  $m = (a_{n-1} + b_{n-1})/2$, depending on the value of f(m), set the value of a_n, b_n

Practice

- When x = a in the differentiable function y = f(x), the tangent line equation is

  y - f(a) = f'(a)(x-a)

  This tangent line meets the x axis when

  x = a - f(a)/f'(a)

  If you repeat this, x will gradually come closer to f(x)=0. With this method, write a program that calculates the root of x^2 - x = 0

```
int newton(float x, float *root)
{
   while (1) {
      if (abs(f(x)) <= EPS) {*root = x; return 0;}
      if (abs(fd(x)) <= EPS) return -1;
      x = x - f(x) / fd(x);      // fd(x): f'(x)
   }
}
```

Ref.

- This method is called the Newton method
- If the derivative is 0, this method will not work

KeyPoints

How do you set the initial value?

Output

GUESS??

1) Find the relation between the Fibonacci sequence and the where the leaves form

2) Find the importance of the "golden ratio". Find the relation between the horizontal and vertical side of the Parthenon.

3) The general term of Fibonacci Sequence can be clearly expressed with mathematics. Compare the resulted values from the equation and the iteration.

Project 13

The Coding Strategy for Troubleshooting

Array and Image

Project Description

Write a program that counts the sum of the squares that are colored in from the smiling face favicon in the 16×16 grid.

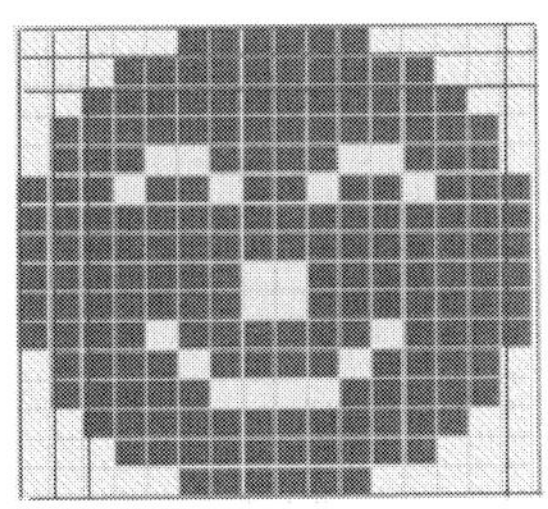

Main Concepts

Favicon

The icon that shows on the address bar in a web browser

(Reference: http://www.favicon.cc/)

Array

Data structure that holds similar data under one name

```
int array_name[12];
```

- Name : `array_name`
- Size(Number of elements that form the array) : 12
- index : 0, 1, 2, 3, ... ,11
- element : `array_name[k]`, k=0,...,11, each element is an independent variable

Main Objectives

- Array concept : relations between array and image
- Repetitive task and array modification
- Modularity

13.01 Figuring out the size of the favicon

Array

- Size = 5, Name = `array`, Value = one-dimensional array of integer

```
int  array[5];
```

data	1	2	3	4	5
index	0	1	2	3	4

- Size = 2×5, Name = array, Value = two-dimensional array of integer

```
int array[2][5];
```

  - `array[1][3]` points at where 9 is saved
  - 1 is the index of the column, and 3 is the index of the row

0	1	2	3	4	5
1	6	7	8	9	10
index	0	1	2	3	4

- `int favicon[16][16];`
  - the size is 16×16, Name = `favicon`, Value = integer
  - Dimension = two-dimensional array of 256 integers

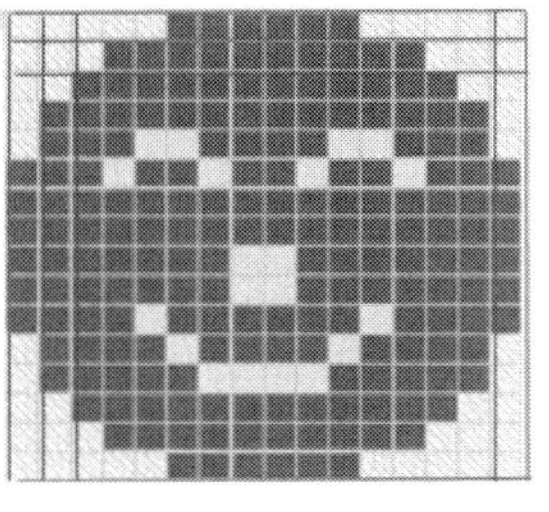

Practice

※ Project Completion

- After creating a new project, add and code the new item main.cpp
- Copy favicon.cpp and favicon.h to the project folder
- Add as existing item to the Solution Explorer
  - add favicon.cpp to the solution source file
  - add favicon.h to the solution header file

※ Relation between Array and Image

- Check if the favicon and the two-dimensional array 1s that were defined by the favicon.cpp are the same
- After Running, compare the number of 1s and the output value
- `ColoredPixel (int row, int column)` run after editing
  - Change BLACK to WHITE

KeyPoints

+ Array and Graph paper

- graph paper = array
- grid = element
- Grid location = column/row

+ Array

Collecting several variables under one name, and distinguishing each variable with indexing

Output

13.02 Writing a code that modifies array

Array modification centered around iteration of row and column

- Model of a code that modifies each element of the two-dimensional array

```
for(row = 0; row < ROWSIZE; row++) {
     for(column = 0 ; column < COLUMNSIZE; column ++) {
          array[row][column] Modifying code
     }
}
```

- Model of a code that modifies the diagonal element of the two-dimensional array

```
for(row = 0; row < ROWSIZE; row++) {
   for(column = 0 ; column < COLUMNSIZE; column ++) {
       if(row == column)
         array[row][column] Modifying code
   }
}
```

Practice

Code test that outputs the array

* Edit `main()` to call `PrintFavicon()` and execute

  `PrintFavicon();` add

* Declare `PrintFavicon()` in favicon.cpp and execute

```
void PrintFavicon()
{
    int row;
    for(row = 0; row < ROWSIZE; row++) {
        printf("%s\n", favicon[row]);
    }
}
```

* Add `PrintFavicon()` prototype to favicon.h and execute

  ▸ `void PrintFavicon();`

* Deleting `\n` from `printf("%s\n")` and execute

KeyPoints

+ Range of index value for column/row

- 0 and above
- up to (size-1)
- otherwise error

+ Prototype

- There is only the head but no body of the function
- The head ends with ';'
- It is required when you call before defining the function

Output

GUESS??

1) Can you save integer values on some elements and save `char` values on some other elements in an array?

2) What happens when index value goes beyond the saving space?
For example, if you define `int array[3];` and run `array[-1] = 1;` or `array[3] = 1;` how would the program react?

3) What are somethings around us that are possible to show with arrays?

4) A bitmap font is a font where the letters appears as it has been colored with pixels on the graph paper. Search on wikipedia.com for the bitmap font.

5) Similar to the bitmap font, there is 7–segment. How is it different from the graph paper and bitmap font? And where is the 7–segment primarily used?

Project 14

Area Estimation by Monte Carlo Method

Project Description

Write a program that calculates the area of the simple closed curve on a plane. (below is the result of the area of the face of favicon)

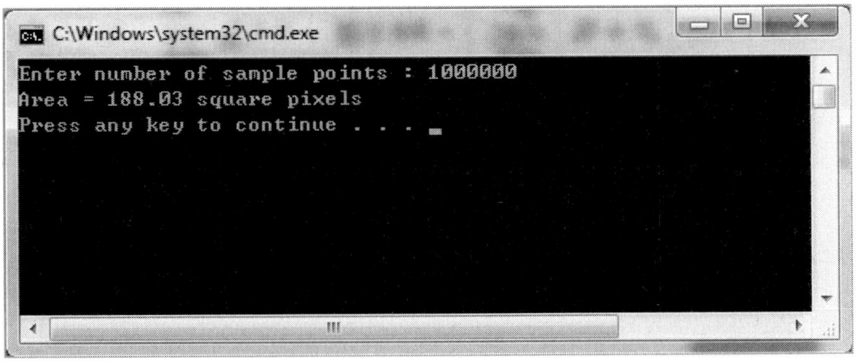

Main Concepts

Monte Carlo Method

The Monte Carlo Method is a method when there are N amount of random numbers (x, y), 0 <= x <= X-1, 0 <= y <= Y-1 and the random numbers inside the simple closed curve is 'a many numbers' you assume the inner area of the simple closed curve is (X * Y) * (a / N)

Simple Closed Curve

A simple closed curve is a curve that forms with the starting point also being the ending point and there are no other points that intersect; like circles, ovals, triangle, which are polygons.

Main Objective

- Repetitive task
- Generating and using random numbers
- Understanding arrays (initializing, modifying)
- Necessity of prototype
- Program modularity (increase independency and re-usability of the source file)

14.01 Completing a Program that Calculates the Area of the Image

Program Flow

<table>
<tr><td colspan="2">Declare variable</td></tr>
<tr><td colspan="2">Generate Image (or Array)</td></tr>
<tr><td rowspan="2">Calculate the Area</td><td>input the sample numbers that will be generated for calculating the area</td></tr>
<tr><td>Find percentage of the simple closed curve out of the total area, then multiply this value to the total area</td></tr>
<tr><td colspan="2">Output the Result</td></tr>
</table>

Practice

Completing the project with the following steps and execute

※ Completing the Project

- Copy the source file favicon.h and favicon.cpp to the project folder
- Refer to the lecture on `main()` and complete
- Implement function `ByMonteCalro()` above function `main()`

※ After executing the program, Input the values below as sample numbers.

- 100
- 1,000
- 1,000,000
- What happens to the accuracy as the sample number increases?

※ The function defined after calling requires its own prototype.

- When `ByMonteCarlo()` is moved below `main()`
- When `ByMonteCarlo()` is moved below `main()`, and the prototype is added above `main()`

```
double ByMonteCarlo(int numOfSamples);
```

- When the definition of `ByMonteCarlo()` is set between the prototype and `main()`

KeyPoints

+ Prototype

- There is only the head but no body of the function
- The head ends with ';'
- It is required when you call before defining the function
- declare the prototype in the header file

+ Sample number and Monte Carlo

- As the sample number increases, it gets closer to a more accurate value
- It does not affect the Monte Carlo if the sample number increases to a certain degree

Output

14.02 Modularizing the Project Source File

⊚ Modularizing the Program File

- Put the re-usable function and it's related functions in to one or more files and make these files as independent as possible
- ByMonteCarlo() is a program with the following characteristics
  - Function definition is made on a separate .c(.cpp) file not in the main.cpp
  - The prototypes of the functions of the .cpp files are collected and made into a .h header file
  - use **#include "header file name"** when this function is used

Practice

Implement the **ByMonteCarlo()** function with a separate source file

※ Implement ByMonteCarlo.cpp and ByMonteCarlo.h

- Add ByMonteCarlo.cpp as a new item to the solution explorer source file
- Add ByMonteCarlo.h as a new item to the solution explorer header file
- ByMonteCarlo.cpp Completion
  - header file #include <stdio.h>, <stdlib.h>, <time.h>, "favicon.h" etc.
  - Move ByMonteCarlo() function from main.cpp
- ByMonteCarlo.h Completion

```
#ifndef __BYMONTECARLO_H_
#define __BYMONTECARLO_H_
double ByMonteCarlo(int numOfSample);
#endif
```

- clean up main.cpp
  - Delete unnecessary things
    - Delete #include <time.h>
    - ByMonteCarlo() Delete prototype declaration
  - Add #include "ByMonteCarlo.h"

KeyPoints

+ Header file system

#ifndef __..._
#define __..._
Declarations
#endif
even if you include twice, it only includes once

+ Modularity

The source file size decreases and the independence and re-usability increases, which makes it easier to manage

Output

14.03 Creating a Function Using Parameters that has Multiple Use

⑥ Parameters of function : compare the two functions below

```
■ bool CheckBlack(int row, int column)
  {
        if (favicon[row][column] == BLACK) return true;
        return false;
  }
■ bool CheckColor(int row, int column, char color)
  {
        if (favicon[row][column] == color) return true;
        return false;
  }
```

Note If there is **CheckColor()** there is no need for **CheckWhite()** which check for **WHITE**

Practice

Calculating the area of the eyes, nose, mouth of favicon

✻ Image Edit
- ▸ #define the color of "favicon.h"
  `#define EYES 'E'` etc.
- ▸ Edit the array of favicon's eyes, nose, mouth to the relevant character in the favicon.cpp

✻ Edit the ByMonteCarlo() to calculate the area that is recognized with color
- ▸ Edit (refer below) ByMonteCarlo.cpp, ByMonteCarlo.h

```
double ByMonteCarlo(int numOfSample, char color);
CheckColor(row, column, color)
```

✻ Edit main() and execute
- ▸ Edit ByMonteCarlo() call to calculate the area of the eyes

```
area = ByMonteCarlo(numOfSample,EYES) * TotalSection();
```

✻ Calculate the area of the nose and mouth with a similar method

KeyPoints

+ Parameter of function
- increase usage of function
- deciding the parameter is very difficult

+ Header file
- Write #include so it can be used where it's needed (i.e.: if the colors are defined in favicon.cpp how can you implement main() ?)

Output

GUESS??

1) Calculate the value ... of pi $\pi = 3.1415$ with the Monte Carlo Method (search wikipedia.com)

2) Think of a way to calculate the value of definite integral with the Monte Carlo method.

3) What are some problems that can be calculated with the Monte Carlo method?

Project 15

The Coding Strategy for Troubleshooting

Searching and Sorting

Project Description

Write a program that calculates and outputs the location (index) of the keyboard input value on the array of function. Also, when the input value does not exist on the array, output the following message "not found".

Main Concepts

Sequential search

A method of searching that matches and checks each element with the searched value. In a size n array, the index searches from 0 to n-1 and compares each element with the searched value.

Binary search

A method of searching that speeds up the search by halving the range of search. It compares the search with the value in the center of the sorted array.

Sort

A process of rearranging date according to a certain sequence.

There are numerous methods of sorting.

Main Objective

- Understanding and manipulating search algorithms(sequential, binary)
- Understanding and manipulating sorting algorithm: bubble sort
- Repetitive task in array
- Initializing the array at declaration point

15.01 Completing a Search Program

◎ Flow of function **main()**

Declare Variable
Output array initialization and array element
Accept input value
Search (Sequential or Binary)
Output search result

Practice

Complete the project with the following steps and execute

✻ Completing the Project

- Create project
- Copy arraylist.cpp, arraylist.h, search.cpp, search.h to project folder
- Add item to the solution explorer
  - Add main.cpp as new item in source file
  - Add search.cpp, arraylist.cpp as existing item in source file
  - Add search.h, arraylist.h as existing item in header file
- Coding main.cpp, search.cpp
  - code `seqsearch()`, `binSearch()` to search.cpp
  - code search.h

✻ Input different values and check if the output is correct

- Input value that exist in the array
- Input value that does not exist in the array

KeyPoints

+ **search**
  - sequential
  - binary
+ **sort**
  - bubble
  - insertion
  - quick
  - etc

Output

15.02 Understanding Sequential Search

◎ Understanding Sequential Search Algorithm

```
for (cursor = 0; cursor < size; cursor++) {
    if (list[cursor] == target) {
        return cursor;
    }
}
return -1; // means data does not exist
```

Practice

Understanding sequential search algorithm with debugger

✻ Run Debugger

- Set the following break point, run debugger, input value that exists in array.
  `result = seqSearch(GetList(), GetSize(), target);`
- Go inside function `seqSearch()` with F11
- After adding `cursor`, `target`, `list[cursor]` to watch window, process with F10 until `return` statement

✻ Repeat the process above with a value that does not exist in array

✻ Initializing Array

- `fillArrayRnd()` of `main()`; change call statement to comment statement
- Modify `int list[NUM_ELEMENT] = {0}` of arraylist.cpp;
  - Initialize as declaring
    `int list[NUM_ELEMENT] = { 3, 2, 5, . . . };`
  - Trace after coding with two cases
  - The number of values inside { } is less than NUM_ELEMENT
  - The number of values inside { } is greater than NUM_ELEMENT
- Run

KeyPoints

+ Initializing Array

- specify value in { }
- if you don't have enough numbers fill in with 0
- If the number of values are greater than the size of the array, there will be more errors

+ Worst case scenario for sequential search

- Searching for value that does not exist in the array

Output

15.03 Understanding Binary Search

Binary Search Algorithm

```
first = 0;
last = size-1;
while (1) {
   if (first > last) break;
   mid = (first + last) / 2;
   if (target > list[mid])
       first = mid + 1;
   else if (target < list[mid])
       last = mid - 1;
   else
       return mid;
}
return -1; // means data does not exist
```

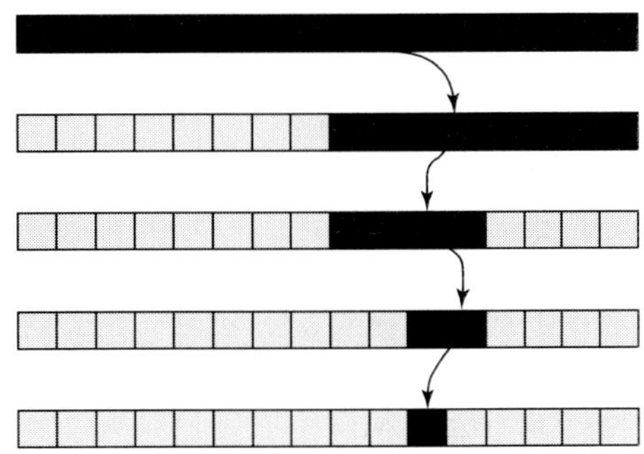

Practice

Editing the program with the following steps and execute

* Run after editing main() to call binSearch()

- Modify seqSearch() call to binarySearch() call
  - process as comment result = seqSearch(GetList(), GetSize(), target);
  - Add result = binarySearch(GetList(), GetSize(), target);
- Input value existing and non-existing in the array after execution

  Ref. The search result can be correct but it can also be wrong

KeyPoints

+ **Binary search speed**
  - $\log_2(n)$
  - with one comparison, the amount of data halves

Output

Practice

* Find out why the `binSearch()` cannot find the accurate value with the debugger
  - Set break point in `binarySearch()` call statement
  - Input value after running debugger
  - Press F11 when you reach the break point and go inside `binarySearch()`
  - Process with F10 and track the value of the primary variable until reaching `return` statement (use watch window)

* Fill array with sorted data and execute
  - Instead of `fillArrayRnd();` call `fillArraySeq();`
  - Using the debugger, check if the output is always correct with any input value.

Output

15.04 Understanding Bubble Sort

Bubble Sort Algorithm

```
for (last = size-1; last >= 1; last--) {
   for(k = 0; k <= last-1; k++) {
      if(list[k] > list[k+1]) {
         tmp = list[k];
         list[k] = list[k+1];
         list[k+1] =tmp;
      }
   }
}
```

Practice

Perform binary search after sorting the array filled of random numbers with `bubbleSort()`

* Edit Program

- main.cpp Edit

```
int main()
{
   fillArrayRnd();
   showElement();
   bubbleSort(GetList(), GetSize());
   printf("--- after bubble sort ---\n");
   showElement();
}
```

- Code `bubbleSort()` function in search.cpp
- Add prototype of `bubbleSort()` to search.h

KeyPoints

+ Number of executions of comparisons

= performance of algorithm

(i.e.) Performance of Bubble sort

Number of Data : n

Number of comparison: $O(n^2)$

it is a slow algorithm

Output

Practice

※ Check the output value of sorted array after running program.

※ Trace bubble sort algorithm with debugger

- Set break point within `bubbleSort()`
- After executing with F5, process with F10 until `return` statement

※ Measure the number of executions of the `if` statement when you sort 5 data with bubble sort

- Create array of 5 data (change to `#define NUM_ELEMENT 5`)
- Measure the number of executions of the `if` statement using the debuggers until the sorting finishes
  - add `int count=0;`
  - Add `count ++;` above `if(list[k] > list[k+1])`
  - when the sorting ends
    `printf("size = %d, count = %d\n",size, count);`

Output

GUESS??

1) What kind of searching method do we use in real life? Do we use sequential search when we look up words in the dictionary? What kind of method do we use to find the biggest apple in a box of apples?

2) What happens when you apply binary search to data that is not sorted?

3) How many comparisons are required to sort 1,000,000 data with bubble sort? If there is a computer that can compare 100,000 data per second, how much time does it require to sort 1,000,000 data with bubble sort?

4) Sorting is a basic algorithm in data handling. For this reason, C provides a sorting function in its library. What kind of methods are there and how does it sort? How much faster is this method compared to bubble sort? Compare how long each takes to sort 10,000 randomly generated data.

5) Data is composed of a collection of different values into one, rather than being composed of one value only. For example, in a contacts list each person's information is composed of name, address, phone number, etc. How would you express a person's information in the C language? If you were to sort the contacts list, which value should you base the sorting?

Project 16

Finding IP address of internet domain name

Project Description

Write a program that takes the domain names and IP addresses in DDN(Dotted Decimal Notation) and saves it on the host table. The picture below shows an example of the program execution.

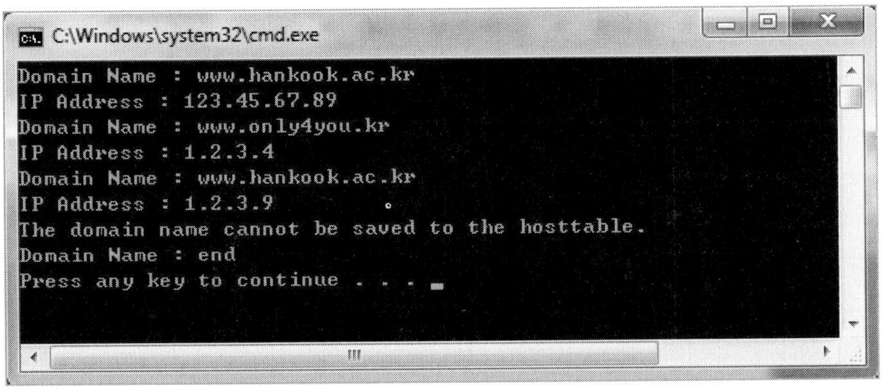

Main Concepts

Structure(**struct**)

- A data type that is used to place a list of highly-related variables (member variables) under one block of memory, making it easy to access and maintain the variables.
- Declaring a **struct** in C language

```
struct {
    char domainname[NAMELENGTH];    // member 1
    char ddnIP[DDNLENGTH];          // member 2
}
```

- **domainname**, **ddnIP** : "member" variables

  All member variables are treated as independent variables.

DDN(Dotted Decimal Notation)

A method in which one value is divided into multiple numbers and separated by dots("."). For example, a 32 bit IPv4 address can be expressed by 4 8bit(0~255) numbers with dots between them

e.g.: 123.45.67.89

Main Objectives

- Structure(**struct**) declaration and initialization
- Table structure searci
- String operations such as **strtok()**, **strcmp()**

16.01 Deriving and coding the program structure

◎ Deriving the program structure

- Program key functions
  - Save host information in a host table and output the table upon termination.
- Hints for deciding the program structure: host and host table.

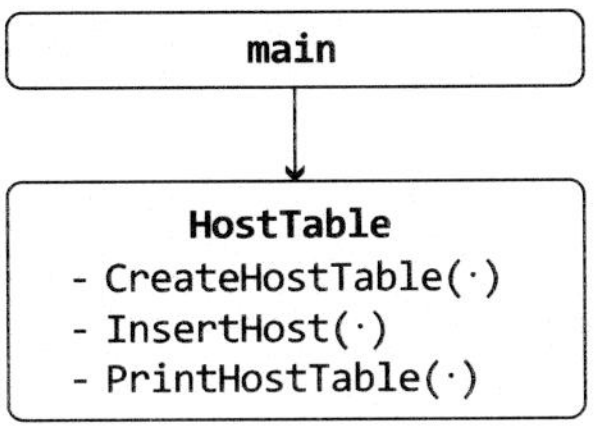

Practice

Follow the steps to complete and run the project

✻ Create a new project

✻ Add main.cpp to the project and progressively expand the project

▸ Start writing main.cpp

- Add #include "HostTable.h" and HostTable.h to the header files in the solution explorer

▸ Write main()

- When writing a function that modifies HostTable, declare function prototype in HostTable.h

(e.g.)
```
void CreateHostTable();
int  InsertHost(char*, char*);
void PrintHostTable();
```

✻ Add HostTable.cpp to the project as a new item then write code

▸ Write each prototype declared functions one-by-one in HostTable.h (start by copying the provided code)

✻ Try various test cases and check the outputs

KeyPoints

✚ Structure Diagram

- Diagram that indicate the relationship between modules

✚ Point to extract structure

- Extract interesting target of the problem
  1) Host
  2) Host table

Output

16.02 Utilizing **struct** and **typedef**

```
#define NAMELEN 256
typedef struct {
    char  name[NAMELEN];
    int   age;
} tPERSON;
int main(void)
{
    tPERSON  person;                                           // S01
    printf("Enter name : "); scanf("%s", person.name);         // S02
    printf("Enter age  : "); scanf("%d", &person.age);         // S03
    printf("name : %s\n", person.name);                        // S04
    printf("age  : %d\n", person.age);                         // S05
    return 0;
}
```

Practice

Use the program above to run these procedures

* Check if the input value outputs correctly

* Modify the `main()` to test these 3 cases below
  - Delete `person.` from lines S02~S05
  - add `char addr[ADDRLEN];` to the structure as a new member variable(also add input and output commands for addr)
  - Change S01 to `tPERSON person, per2;`(i.e., add `per2`)
    After S03, add `per2 = person;`
    From S04 and S05, change `person.` to `per2.`

* Replace `int` and `char` with user-defined types
  - type definition : `typedef int INT;`
    `typedef char CHAR;`
  - Replace all instances of `int` and `char` with `INT` and `CHAR`

KeyPoints

+ typedef

- Defining user-defined types
- Allows the reuse of types, which simplifies programs
- tPERSON is a user-defined type
- tPERSON person]; is same as
  struct {
    char name[. .];
    int age;
  } person;

+ per2=person;

- Copies all member variables of person to per2

Output

16.03 Creating reliable HostTable

Detecting and handling table overflow

Putting data into tables without checking its availability can cause serious errors

Handling table overflow

```
int InsertHost(char *name, char *ip)
{
   if (next >= TABLESIZE) {
      return -1;  // handling error
   }
   strcpy(hosttable[next].domainname, name);
   strcpy(hosttable[next].ddnIP, ip);
   next++;
   return 0;
}
```

Practice

※ Revise the code to prevent adding more data when the host table runs out of space

- Add code to `InsertHost()`
- Prevent adding more hosts than allowed by the table size

※ Prevent inserting multiple hosts with same name

- Implement `bool FindName(char *name)` - use sequential search
- Modify `InsertHost()` to only add a host after verfying with `FindName()` that the host is not already in the table

```
if (FindName(name)==true)
    return -1;
```

※ Track how many hosts are saved in `hosttable`

- Increment the number of hosts after every successful Insert
  - Declare `static int number;` and add `number++;` to `InsertHost()`
  - Output number from `PrintHostTable()`

KeyPoints

+ Array index

- 0 or bigger
- array size - 1

+ string operation functions

- strcmp : comparison
- strcpy : copying
- strlen : length
- <string.h> is required

Output

16.04 Converting an IP address in DDN to a 32bit integer

⑥ Test Program

```
#include <stdio.h>
#include <stdlib.h>   // required for atoi()
#include <string.h>   // required for strtok()

#define  DDNLENGTH 30

int main(void)
{
   char             ip[DDNLENGTH], *str;
   unsigned int     ip32 = 0;

   printf("Enter IP : ");
   scanf("%s", ip);

   str = strtok(ip, ".");         // Seperate the string ip by "."
   ip32 = atoi(str);

   while(1) {
      str = strtok(NULL,".");     // from here, use NULL as the first
                                     parameter of strtok()
      if(str == NULL) break;
      ip32 = (ip32 << 8) + atoi(str);
   }

   return 0;
}
```

Practice

* Use the debugger to monitor program behaviour for the test cases below

0.0.0.1	0.0.1.0	0.1.0.0	1.0.0.0	1.0.0.1
1.2.3	1.2.3..	1.2.3.4.5	..1.2.3.4	

* Modify the program to find the last number and print it
  - `char *last;` // Declare a placeholder variable
  - `last = str;` // Add this line to an appropriate place
  - `printf("Last digit : %s \n", last);`

* Copy in advance in case the input string cannot be revised
  - Print `ip` right before `return`
    add `printf("ip = %s \n", ip);` to observe the changing values of `ip`

KeyPoints

+ Integer
- declare as unsigned int

+ strtok()
- Split a string using a specified delimiter. Modifies the original string. Calling method is important.

+ a<<8
- Execute bitwise left shift 8 times
- Same as a*256
  << : left shift
  >> : right shift

+ atoi(str)
- convert string to an integer!

Output

GUESS??

1) How does the DNS decide IP addresses?

2) How can you find out the domain name and IP address for Ajou University?

3) What is the IP address for the computer that you are using?

4) Can each user allocate their own IP addresses? Is there an agency or organization that allocates IP addresses?

5) Are IP address fixed or can they be changed?

6) How many IP address can be generated using 32bit IP address? Can all the computers around the world (connected to the internet) be identified using 32bit IP address?

Project 17

Creating and Reading Bit Map File

Project Description

Convert the image data that is saved in an array to a BMP file. Also, read the information in the generated BMP file into another array, and verify whether the data stored in these two arrays are the same.

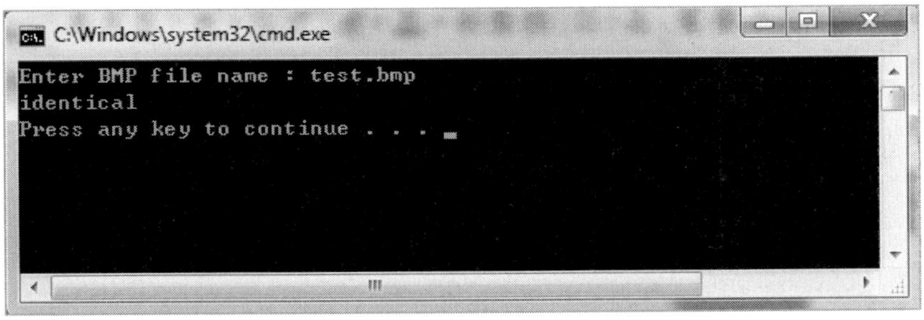

Main Concepts

Bitmap file

A format for saving an image to a file

- The extension for bitmap files is .BMP
- Bitmap files are consisted of header and image area, and the header contains general information of the image properties(e.g., file size)

Pixel

- Indicates picture element. Corresponds to a sample in a raster image
- In general, each pixel in an image is expressed using more than one byte. Colors of pixels in an image are specified in RGB(red, green, blue) or CMYB(cyan, magenta, yellow, black) format.

Main Objectives

- ✎ Save and read bitmap files(.bmp)
- ✎ Comparing arrays and the significance of array names
- ✎ How arrays are saved in memory devices
- ✎ One-dimensional arrays and two-dimensional arrays

17.01 Creating and reading bitmap files

main.cpp

```
#include  <stdio.h>
#include  "imageArray.h"

#define FILENAMELENGTH  256

int main(void)
{
   char    filename[FILENAMELENGTH];
   int     same;

   CreateImage();

   printf("Enter BMP file name : ");
   scanf("%s", filename);

   SaveGiven2DImage(filename);
   Load2DImageFile(filename);
   same = CompareTwo2DImages();

   if (same == 1)     printf("same\n");
   else               printf("different\n");

   return 0;
}
```

Practice

Creating, executing, and verifying the result of the program

- Create the project and copy these files to the project folder `SimpleBMP.cpp,SimpleBMP.h,imageArray.cpp,imageArray.h`
- Add main.cpp as a new item to source files in the solution explorer and write code
- Add SimpleBMP.cpp and imageArray.cpp to source files as existing items, and add SimpleBMP.h and imageArray.h to header files as existing items
- Run the program(use "out.bmp" as the file name), and check the "out.bmp" file with the windows paint
- Change the value of `BLACK` or `WHITE` to a number between 0~255(e.g., 67) and run the program again

Ref. the provided program uses values between 0 and 255 for colors

```
#define NumBitsPerPixel       8
pDst->biBitCount = NumBitsPerPixel;
```

KeyPoints

+ **Program source**
  - .cpp: functions/variables
  - .h: prototypes and others
+ **Program structures**
  - consists of multiple independent files

Output

17.02 Comparing elements and names of two arrays

main.cpp

```
int  image[SIZE];
```

- Declaring an array
  reserves space in a memory storage for storing `SIZE` integers
- Name of an array = address of a memory storage. i.e., value of `image` = address of the save point of beginning of values

Practice

Compare two arrays as follows

✻ Implement a function to compare arrays by their names

- Implement `CompareTwo2DImagesbyName(void)` in imageArray.cpp

```
int CompareTwo2DImagesbyName(void)
{
   if (image2D == imagefromBMP2D)
      return 1;
   return 0;
}
```

- Add prototype for the function in imageArray.h
- In `main()`, call `CompareTwo2DImagesbyName()`

```
if(CompareTwo2DImagesbyName()==1) printf("same\n");
else printf("different\n");
```

- Execute the program and check the output displays "same", followed by "different"

Output

KeyPoints

+ Name value of arrays

- Different arrays are stored in different locations and addresses, resulting in different name value of arrays
- As a result, to compare arrays, you must compare all elements of arrays one-by-one

+ Debugger Watch Window

- Appears at the bottom when running with the debugger
- If not visible, enable by clicking 'Debug' > 'Windows' > 'Watch' from the menus
- Add new variables or equations in empty lines

Practice

※ Analyze reason for the output

- Set a break point at `if (image2D == imagefromBMP2D)`
- Press F5 to run the program in debugging mode
- Use "out.bmp" as the output file name and run the program to the break point
- Add array names `image2D` and `imagefromBMP2D` to the watch window
- Compare the values in the watch window

Output

17.03 bmp file modification considering bitmap file image coordinates

Image array and bitmap file image storage

Image stored in `char image2D[RSIZE][CSIZE];` and in bmp file

array image	bitmap file bgImage
1st column `image2D[0]`	last column `image2D[RSIZE-1]`
2nd column `image2D[1]`	. . .
. . .	2nd column `image2D[1]`
last column `image2D[RSIZE-1]`	1st column `image2D[0]`

Practice

✻ Modify a part of the image array and re-run the program (Ref. The image shown on paint is upside-down with the image shown on the array)

✻ Revise the code to reverse the image array before saving and reading

- Modification
  - Change `MoveImage2DArray2BMP()`, `MoveBMP2Image2DArray()` to put last item first to `bmp->bgImage`
- `MoveImage2DArray2BMP()`

```
for (line=Wy-1,bmpLine=0;line>=0;line--,bmpLine++)
    for (column = 0; column < Wx; column++)
        bmp->bgImage[bmpLine*lineSize+column]=
            p[line][column];
```

- `MoveBMP2Image2DArray()`

```
for(line=Wy-1,bmpLine=0;line>=0;line--,bmpLine++)
    for(column=0; column<Wx; column++)
        p[line][column] =
            bmp->bgImage[bmpLine*lineSize+column];
```

✻ After modifying the image, verify if the image is saved correctly

KeyPoints

+ **image file**
  Image arrays are inverted before being saved as image files

+ **Inverting image arrays before reading from or saving as image files makes handling them more intuitive**

Output

17.04 Two-dimensional array operations

◎ Two-dimensional array

```
char image2D[2][3];
```

- `image2D` : the address where 2*3 `char` variables are saved
- `image2D[k]` : the address where the array `image2D[k][0]` is saved
- `image2D[k][m]` : the value saved in `image2D[k][m]`

Test program

```
#include <stdio.h>

char image2D[2][3] = { {1, 2, 3}, {4, 5, 6} };

int main(void)
{
    printf("image2D                   = %d\n", image2D);
    printf("image2D[0]                = %d\n", image2D[0]);
    printf("image2D[1]                = %d\n", image2D[1]);
    printf("image2D[1][1]             = %d\n", image2D[1][1]);
    printf("image2D[1]-image2D[0]     = %d\n", image2D[1]-image2D[0]);

    return 0;
}
```

Practice

Testing key attributes of a two-dimensional array

✻ Implement a new project with the test program and execute

- Predict the meaning of output value and how it is related to memory storage
- Check why the values of `image2D` and `image2D[0]` are identical
- Verify `image2D[1] - image2D[0]` is equal to 3, the size of each column

✻ Change `image2D` into a 3x4 array and test with the debugger

- Set a break point at the first instance of `printf`
- Run with the debugger and check values of this variables with the watch window
  - `image2D`
  - `image2D[0]`, `image2D[1]`, `image2D[2]`
  - `image2D[1]-image2D[0]`, `image2D[2]-image2D[1]`
  - `image2D[0][0]`, `image2D[0][3]`, `image2D[2][0]`, `image2D[2][3]`

KeyPoints

- The name of the two-dimensional array
- The address where the two-dimensional array starts
- image[0]: the address where the row 0 starts
- image[0][0]: the value stored in row 0, column 0

Output

17.05 Converting an image into a one-dimensional array

◎ One-demensional array

- Declared and handled as they are stored in memory devices
- Calculating an index is complicated

  e.g. Converting a two-dimensional array index to a one-dimensional array index
  Consider a one-dimensional array
  `char image[ImageRows * ImageColumns] = { . . . };`
  and a two-dimensional array
  `char image2D[ImageRows][ImageColumns];`
  In this case,
  `image2D[row][col]` is equal to `image[row * ImageColumns + col]`

- One-dimensional arrays are easier to pass arguments of functions

  e.g. Functions usin two-dimensional arrays as arguments have to be declared like below

```
MoveImage2DArray2BMP(tBMP *bmp,
                     BYTE p[ImageRows2D][ImageColumns2D],
                     int Wx, int Wy)
```

  The number of rows and columns must be specified,
  e.g. `BYTE p[ImageRows2D][ImageColumns2D]`

  e.g. One-dimensional arrays can simply use *

```
MoveImageArray2BMP(tBMP *bmp, BYTE *p, int Wx, int Wy)
```

Practice

* Modifying `imageArray.cpp`
  - `image`, `imagefromBMP` declaration and initialization
  - Implement `LoadBMP2Image(char *fn)`
  - Implement `SaveImage2BMP(char *fn)`
  - Implement `compareTwoImages()`
    (Refer to `CompareTwoImages()` and compare each element of two-dimensional arrays)
* Modify main.cpp
  - Replace old functions with new ones
* Check the result of execution

KeyPoints

+ **How to prevent errors and write code faster**
  - what you see = code
  - as simple as possible
+ **High-dimensional arrays are dificult to pass as arguments of functions**
+ **Two-dimensional arrays and function parameter**

Output

GUESS??

1) Microsoft Windows provides various programs for opening bitmap files. What are they?

2) How many bits are required to express a black-and-white image pixel?

3) How many bits are required to express a colored image pixel? How does number of bits in a pixel affect detailed levels of colors?

4) How do colors change as their RGB values change? What values of R, G, B create black?

5) Why is it necessary to know number of rows and columns in a function using two-dimensional arrays as an argument?

Project 18

The Coding Strategy for Troubleshooting

Pattern Creation

Project Description

Write a program that creates a repeat pattern by copying a pattern defined in a rectangular area to another area in the same array, and saves the repeat pattern to a bitmap file. The screenshot below shows the program execution, the source file source.bmp, and the output file out.bmp.

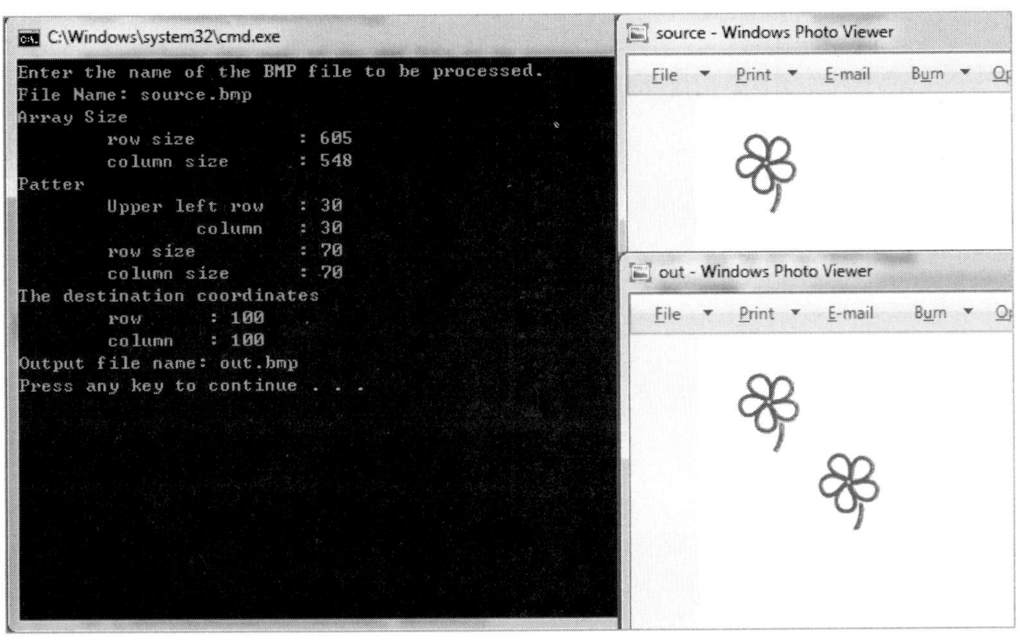

Main Concepts

Pattern / Repeat pattern

- [http://www.artyfactory.com/repeat-patterns/]
- Pattern : a repeated form of design such as lines, shapes, tones, and colors
- repeat patterns : an essential skill for all designers
- William Morris : one of the best pattern designer, who described a "good decorative pattern" as:

  "Something that will not drive us into unrest or callousness; something which reminds us of life beyond itself and which has the impress of imagination strong on it; and something which can be done by a great many people and without too much difficulty and with pleasure."

Main Objectives

✎ Copying a part of an array
✎ Creating repeat patterns
✎ Arrays and repetitive tasks

18.01 Creating and reading bitmap files

Practice

Create a new project, complete the project with following steps and execute

- Copy Image.cpp, SimpleBMP.cpp, Image.h, SimpleBMP.h, CopyArea.h, source.bmp to the project folder
- Add Image.cpp, SimpleBMP.cpp, Image.h, SimpleBMP.h, CopyArea.h as existing items
- add main.cpp, CopyArea.cpp to source files in the solution explorer as new items then code
- Before running the program, check the image and the location of pattern of source.bmp
- Ref. The image and the pattern of source.bmp

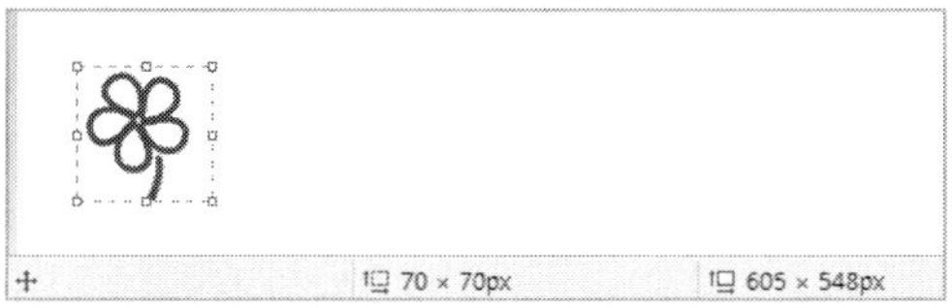

- Execute the program then input the following
  - File name: source.bmp
  - Upper left row: 0, column: 0, Width: 100, height: 100
  - Input target copy location: row: 100, column: 100
  - Output file name: out.bmp
- Open out.bmp and check if the pattern has been copied to the target correctly

Output

Practice

- Copying patterns to multiple places
  - If pattern location or size is -1
  - If one of the target coordinates is -1 or larger than the entire image boundary
  - If the source image file does not exist or is not a bitmap file
  - Copy the pattern to multiple places

Output

18.02 Copying one-dimensional arrays

⑥ A simple program that copies one-dimensional arrays

```
#define  MATSIZE  10
int mat[MATSIZE] = {0, 1, 2, 3, 4, 5, 6, 7, 8, 9};
int main(void)
{
   int k, from, to, last, dest;
   printf(" Enter from last to : ");
   scanf("%d %d %d",&from, &last, &to);
   for (k = from, dest = to; k <= last; k++, dest++)
      mat[dest] = mat[k];
   // mat print
}
```

Practice

Complete the project with the program above and execute

* Run the following test cases to find problems in the program
  - Copy `mat[3]~mat[5]` to `mat[0]~mat[2]`
  - Copy `mat[4]~mat[7]` to `mat[5]~mat[8]`
  - Copy `mat[4]~mat[7]` to `mat[9]~mat[12]`

* Correct the following errors and test the program
  - The program is only able to copy within columns
    - `if (dest < MATSIZE) mat[dest] = mat[k];`
  - Differentiate the cases where `from > to` and `from < to`
    - `if (from > to)` copy from `mat[from]` to `mat[last]`
    - `else` copy from `mat[last]` to `mat[from]`

Output

KeyPoints

+ Precautions for copying
- The direction of copying
- The area of copying

+ Using temporary placeholder, tmp, is simple, but it is slower because the contents will be copied twice

+ memmove
(char*dst, char*src, int number)
- char copy function
- <string.h> is required
- For int arrays, the copying happens (sizeof(int) * number of elements) times

+ sizeof(<type>)
The memory size required to save a variable of <type> type

Practice

* Make sure that the program does not copy if `from`, `to`, or `dest` is out of bounds

* Implement a function to copy a part of `src` to `dst`
  - `void Copy1DArray(int *src, int N, int from, int last, int to);`

* Implement a function `Copy1DArrayTmp` that uses temporary placeholder
  - Copy `mat[from]~mat[last]` to `tmp[from]~tmp[last]`
  - Copy `tmp[from]~tmp[last]` to `mat[to]~mat[to+last-from]`

* Implement a copying function using memmove(destination, source, size)

Output

18.03 Analyzing **CopyArea** which copies parts of two-dimensional arrays

Copying two-dimensional arrays

- Copying a rectangular area within a two-dimensional array
- Rectangular area to be copied : `fromRow`, `lastRow`, `fromCol`, `lastCol`
- Target copy location : `toRow`, `toCol`
- Implement `copyArea()` to copy the one-dimensional arrays in each row

```
if (fromRow > toRow) {// copy rows incrementally
    for (k=fromRow, dest=toRow; k<=lastRow; k++,dest++)
        memmove(&matrix[dest][toCol], &matrix[k][fromCol],
                  lastCol-fromCol+1);
} else {                  // copy rows decrementally
    for (k=lastRow,dest=toRow+lastRow-fromRow;
         k>=fromRow;k--,dest--)
        memmove(&matrix[dest][toCol], &matrix[k][fromCol],
                  lastCol-fromCol+1);
}
```

Practice

✻ Create a separate project to test CopyArea()

- Add main.cpp to test CopyArea()

```
#include "copyArea.h"
#define ROW  3
#define COL  4
int GetRowSize()      { return ROW; }
int GetColumnSize()   { return COL; }
unsigned char image[ROW * COL] =
        { 0, 1, 2, 3, 10, 11, 12, 13, 20, 21, 22, 23};
```

KeyPoints

+ &

- An operator that returns the address of its operand
- &mat[1][2] returns the address of mat[1][2]
- The name of an array returns the address of the first element mat==&mat[0][0]

Output

Practice

- Add CopyArea.cpp and CopyArea.h, and add following code to image.h

```
#define BMP_BYTE unsigned char
extern BMP_BYTE* image;
int GetRowSize();
int GetColumnSize();
```

- Various tests for copying

※ CopyArea has various exception handling implemented in it

- Find the part of program that finds the area to be copied from, make it into comments, and execute the program
  - defined as `fromRow`, `fromCol`, `fromLastRow`, `fromLastCol`
- Test various cases of copying

Output

GUESS??

1) How long would it take for 1GB of memory to be copied?

2) Is it always possible to use temporary placeholder (tmp) in arrays? What can make it difficult to use this technique?

3) How can you define a pattern with figures other than rectangular shapes (triangles, circles, or pentagons) or images? What would happen if the image in the target places for these patterns is deleted?

4) What are some functions, other than `memmove()`, that starts with mem?

Project 19

Designing Recursive Function

Project Description

"Tower of Hanoi"

A puzzle created in 1883 by E. Lucas. Write a program that outputs each step when n number of disks are moved from 'A' to 'B' then 'C'.

The rules are, 1) Only one disk can be moved at a time

2) You cannot stack the bigger disk on top of the smaller disk

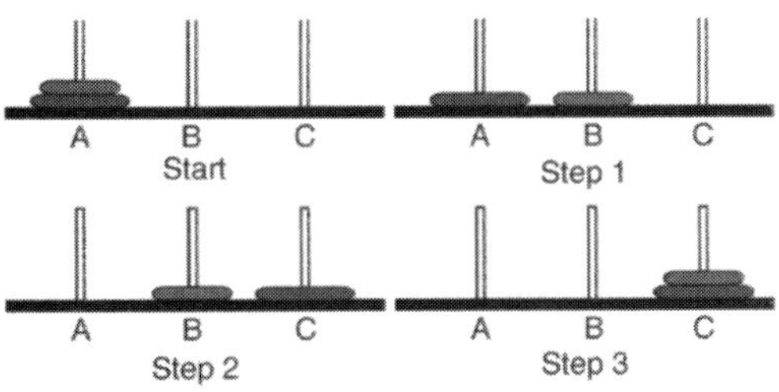

Tower of Hanoi

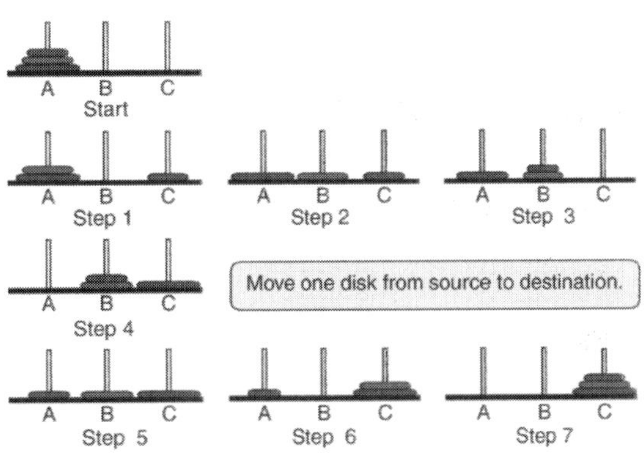

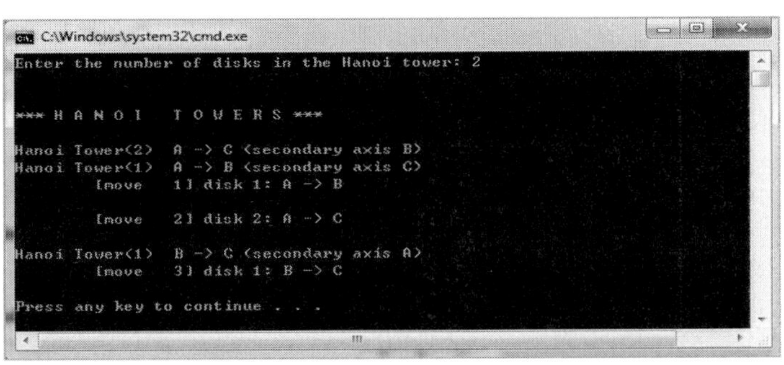


```
Enter the number of disks in the Hanoi tower: 2

*** H A N O I   T O W E R S ***

Hanoi Tower(2)  A -> C (secondary axis B)
Hanoi Tower(1)  A -> B (secondary axis C)
        [move   1] disk 1: A -> B

        [move   2] disk 2: A -> C

Hanoi Tower(1)  B -> C (secondary axis A)
        [move   3] disk 1: B -> C

Press any key to continue . . .
```

Main Concepts

Recursion

Finding the answer Solution(Pbig) of problem Pbig, by using Solution (Psmall) which is the answer for same but smaller problem, Psmall

GCD(6, 21) = GCD(3, 6)

GCD(6, 21) is a bigger problem than GCD(3, 6)

n! = n * (n-1)!

n! is a bigger problem than (n-1)!

Iteration

Repeating same commands over and over

```
for(k = 1; k <= n; k++)
    s += k;
```

is repeated executions of `s += k;`

Main Objectives

- Recursion and iteration
- Problem solving with recursion
- Writing recursive functions

19.01 Creating and running the project

⑨ Hanoi(n, from, to, tmp)

The exit condition of recursion	When number of disks (n) is 1 Move directly from `from` to `to`
Using smaller problems to express the original problem	Move (n–1) disks from `from` to `tmp` `Hanoi(n-1, from, tmp, to);`
	Move n disks from `from` to `to`
	Move (n–1) disks from `tmp` to `to` `Hanoi(n-1, tmp, to, from);`

- Recursion

  To solve `Hanoi(n, from, to, tmp)`, use a smaller problem `Hanoi(n-1, from, tmp, to)`and `Hanoi(n-1, tmp, to, from)`

- The followings are same problems with different sizes

  `Hanoi(n, from, to, tmp)` : size n

  `Hanoi(n-1, from, tmp, to)` : size n-1

  `Hanoi(n-1, tmp, to, from)` : size n-1

Practice

※ Creating project and coding main.cpp

- Write `main()`
- Code Hanoi above `main()`

```
typedef char ROD;
void Hanoi(int n, ROD from, ROD to, ROD, tmp);
```

Output

Practice

* Run the following test cases and examine how the disks move
  - When the number of disks is 1
  - When the number of disks is 2
  - When the number of disks is 3
  - When the number of disks is 4

Output

19.02 Practicing with recursive programs

A typical outline of recursive functions

```
<ValueType>   RecursiveFunction (ProblemSize)
{
     if (ProblemSize <= TheSmallestSize) {
          Directly solve the problem since the size is the smallest;
          return Value;
     }
     NewSize = a size that is smaller than ProblemSize;
     Use combinations of RecursiveFunction(NewSize)
           to solve RecursiveFunction (ProblemSize);
     return Value;
}
```

Practice

✻ Solve the following problem using a recursive function

- Finding the greatest common denominator of two natural numbers (GCD(a, b) = GCD(b, a % b))
- Finding the factorial of a natural number n! = n * (n-1)!

Output

KeyPoints

+ Essential components of recursion

- The exit condition of recursion
- The relationship between small and big problem

(e.g.)
GCD(a, b)=
GCD(b. a % b)
F(n)=n+1.0/F(n-1)

+ Integer division

- modulo calculation

Practice

- Finding the sum of natural numbers from 1 to n
  (S(n) = S(n-1) + n)
- The Fibonacci sequence $F_n = F_{n-1} + F_{n-2}$, and $F_0 = 1$, $F_1 = 1$
- Finding the value of a continued fraction below
  F(n) = n + 1.0 / F(n-1)

$$n+\cfrac{1}{(n-1)+\cfrac{1}{(n-2)+\cfrac{1}{\dots+\cfrac{1}{0+\cfrac{1}{1}}}}}$$

Output

19.03 Observing how a recursive function runs

Function call stack and recursive function execution

- Calculating the sum from 1 to n

```
int Sum2n(int n)
{
    int  tmp;
    if (n<=1) return 1;  // the exit condition
    tmp = Sum2n(n-1);    // using a smaller problem to solve the big
                         // problem
    return tmp + n;
}
```

- When `Sum2n(3)` is called

```
Sum2n(3) → { tmp=Sum2n(2); → { tmp=Sum2n(1); → { return 1; }
                               return tmp+2;
                             }
             return tmp+3;  // 6 is returned
           }
```

Practice

* Analyzing call stack
  - Write a program that uses Sum2n()
  - Set a break point where Sum2n() is called and run the project in debugger
  - From the toolbar, select Debug > Windows > Call Stack
  - Use F11(Step Into) and observe the changes in the call stack window
  - Compare the call stack window and the picture above

Output

KeyPoints

+ **Function call stack**
  - Parameter value
  - return address
  - auto variable
  - 'Call Stack' displays the last function called on top of the window (hence the "stack"), displaying called functions in reverse order
+ **extern/static variables**
  - Not in stack
  - Must be careful when using them in a recursion function

19.04 Counting the number of recursion in a recursive function

⑥ How to count the number of recursion

```
int freq = 0;
<recursive function>( ... )
{
     <declare a local variable>
     freq ++;
     <existing code>
}
```

Practice

※ Counting how many times recursive function Hanoi() is called in the Hanoi program

- Declare int freq = 0; before Hanoi()
- Every time Hanoi() is called, freq++;
- Before main() is returned, output freq
  printf("The number of total recursion = %d\n",freq);

※ Counting how many times the function Fibonacci() is called in the Fibonacci sequence

- Modification
  - Declare freq, and freq++; every time Fibonacci is called
  - In main(), before return, output freq
- Run the program and use 3 as the input
- Run the program and use 6 as the input

KeyPoints

+ Recursive Fibonacci

- Simple recursive algorithm will be called too many times
- An efficient algorithm with minimum recursion is required

Output

Practice

* Performance comparison of a recursive method and an iterative method
  - Implement Fibonacci using the two methods
  - Measure how long it takes to find `Fibonacci(24)` 1,000 times and compare the results
    - `#include <time.h>`
    - Use `time_t TimeStart = clock();` to measure the starting time
    - Use `time_t TimeEnd = clock();` to measure the ending time
    - Interval in seconds : `float TimePerSec = (TimeEnd-TimeStart)/(CLOCKS_PER_SEC);`

Output

GUESS??

1) What are the exit conditions of following recursive functions?

   (1) factorial(int n)

   (2) GCD(int a, int b)

   (3) Hanoi(int n, char src, char dst, char tmp)

2) Does a recursive function always use a smaller problem to solve the bigger problem? Think about a problem of finding an approximate of Pi using the relationship between Pi and continued fraction. What will be the exit condition for a recursive solution?

$$\frac{4}{\pi} = 1 + \cfrac{1}{3 + \cfrac{4}{5 + \cfrac{9}{7 + \cfrac{16}{9 + \cfrac{25}{11 + \cfrac{36}{13 + \ddots}}}}}}$$

3) There is a conceptual difference between reiteration from recursion and from `while` or `for` loops. What is the difference? Can all loops be replaced with recursion? Can all recursion be replaced with `while` or `for` loops?

4) What are the pros and cons of recursive approach?

5) What are the similarities between problems that can be solved by recursion?

Project **20** The Coding Strategy for Troubleshooting

ASCII Art

Project Description

Write a program that converts a black and white bitmap(bmp) image to an ASCII art. If the file does not exist or the program cannot be executed correctly, output an appropriate error message. The picture below shows a bitmap image and converted ASCII art.

```
C:\Windows\system32\cmd.exe
Enter the name of the BMP file : cat.bmp
        Image Size :  Width 1536 pixels, height 1536 pixels
The size of a tile which corresponds to a character string
        Tile width : 15
        Title height : 30
ASCII Art file name : cat.txt
Press any key to continue . . .
```

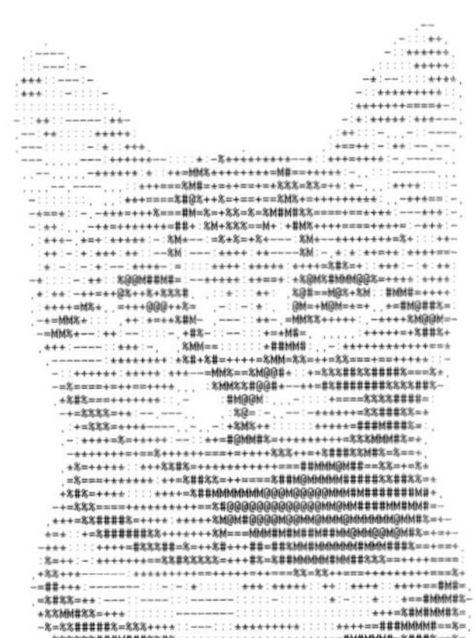

Main Concepts

ASCII art

A method that expresses images with printable ASCII characters. In general, a font with fixed width is used for an ASCII art. Also means Text based visual art.

Main Objectives

- Repeated calculation and array
- Understanding file operations `fopen`, `fgets`, `fclose`
- Calculating data within arrays

20.01 Creating an ASCII art

Isolating developments of core functions in **main**

- A function that reads BMP files

```
int OpenImage(BMPFilename);
```

- A function that converts image files to ASCII arts

```
int GenerateASCIIArt(tileHeight, tileWidth);
```

- A function that saves the ASCII arts to files

```
int SaveASCIIArt(TextFilename);
```

Practice

Creating a project and execute

✻ Creating a project and preparations

- Create a project, and add Image.cpp, SimpleBMP.cpp, ASCIIArt.cpp, Image.h, SimpleBMP.h, ASCIIArt.h, monalisa.bmp, mouse.bmp, images.bmp to project source files folder

✻ Constructing the project and coding

- Add Image.cpp, SimpleBMP.cpp, ASCIIArt.cpp Image.h, SimpleBMP.h, ASCIIArt.h to the project as existing items
- Add main.cpp as a new item and write the code
- Complete ASCIIArt.cpp
- Add following lines to ASCIIArt.cpp as a global variable

```
static char MapASCIIChars[MAPPINGSIZE]
     = { '@','M','#','%','=','+','*',':','-','.',' '};
```

KeyPoints

- The width to height ratio for characters in the command prompt is approximately 1:2
- In effect, the ratio of image pixels horizontally and vertically must be 1:2 to create an ASCII art with less distortion

Output

Practice

※ Create an ASCII art, and check the result with the notepad

- Files: cat.bmp, monarisa.bmp, black.bmp, mouse.bmp
- Tile sizes: 5x10, 15x30, 10x20, 20x40
- Changes in `MapASCIIChars[MAPPINGSIZE]`

Output

20.02 Handling files

5 steps of handling files

- Variable: `FILE *fp;` // must be of `FILE *` type
- Preparation: `fp = fopen(filename,"w" or "r");`
- Writing / Reading

  fprintf(fp, <format>, Variables); or fputs(string, fp);

  fscanf(fp, <format>, Addresses); or

  fgets(string, sizeof(string), fp);
- Inspection

  `feof(fp)` // returns **true** when there is no more data to read; end of file(eof)
- Finalize: `fclose(fp);`

Practice

* Using file operation functions to copy a text file

▸ Creat a new project, add main.cpp and write code

```
int main(void)
{
   char line[ .. . . ];
   FILE *fin = fopen("littlePrince.txt", "r");
   FILE *fout = fopen("copy.txt", "w");
   if (fin==NULL || fout==NULL) { exit(0); }
   while (1) {
      //if there is no more data in fin, break;
      //read from fin, use fgets()
      //output data to screen, use puts()
      //output data to a file(fout), use fprintf() and fputs()
   }
   // finalize using fclose()
   return 0;
}
```

KeyPoints

- commas ',' between commands a=1, b=2; execute a=1 and then execute b=2
- printf(...), exit(0); execute printf and then execute exit(0);
- exit(): exit the program
- gets(): take input string from keyboard, convert '\n' to null character('\0')
- puts(): Converts the null character at the end of a string to '\n' and prints the string
- fgets(), fputs(): keeps the '\n'
- fgets(): adds null character at the end of a string, fputs(): deletes the null character at the end of a string, and prints the string

Practice

- Compare the generated file, test.txt, and "littlePrince.txt"
- Instead of "littlePrince.txt", use a file that does not exist to run the program
- Comment out `fin = fopen(...);` and run the program

Output

GUESS??

1) A lot of ASCII art images, web pages, and a program that converts pictures to ASCII arts can be found by Googling ASCII art. Use them to generate ASCII arts from pictures captured with cameras.

Ref. Use your cell phone to capture an image(e.g. faces of your friends) and do the following

(1) Open the image file with the Windows paint,

(2) Use the 'selection tool' to select the area to be converted,

(3) Use 'crop' tool and 'save as' > BMP image with 'file format' of 256 color bitmap,

(4) Click 'save' to save as a bitmap file

(5) Run the ASCII art program with the bitmap file

2) Text files with same characters can look different if they have different fonts. Find out what are some of the bitmap fonts commonly used in Windows.

3) From the commonly used bitmap fonts, find their area. It is easy to find the areas with the Monte Carlo method.

Project **21**

The Coding Strategy for Troubleshooting

Evaluating Postfix Expression

Project Description

Write a program that calculates the value of a postfix expression. Each input is specified by 'n' or 'o', indicating numerical operand and operator respectively. When 'n' is entered as an input, the program should prompt user to enter an integer operand. Otherwise when 'o' is entered as an input, the program should prompt user to enter '+' or '-' operator. When ';' is entered as an input, the program calculates the postfix expression, outputs the resulting value and terminates the program.

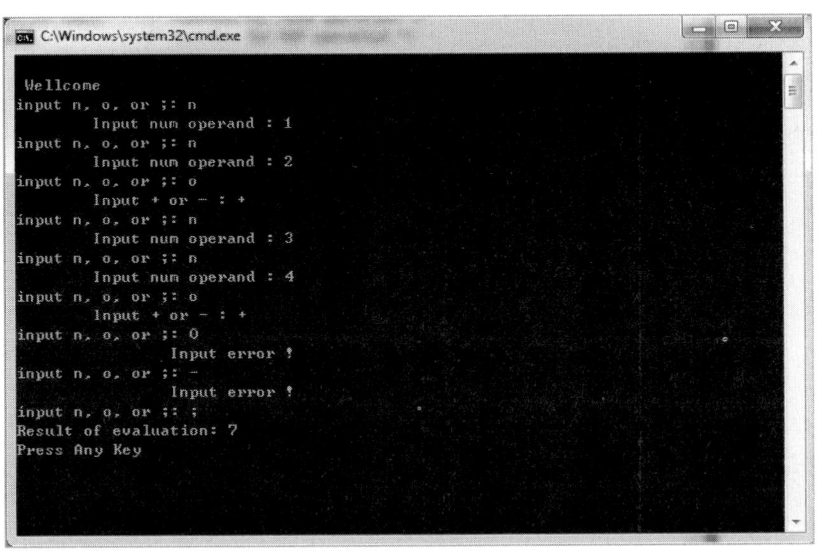

Main Concepts

Postfix notation

A notation for writing arithmetic expressions in which the operands appear before their operators

1 2 +

Stack

A data structure in which data are stacked, resembling a pile of book or dishes. Inserting an item into a stack is called push, and removing the item on the top of a stack is called pop. It is also known as LIFO(Last in First Out) data structure to demonstrate the reverse sequential processing of data.

Main Objectives

- Postfix notation
- Characteristics of stack data structure and its uses
- Evaluating postfix expressions using stack
- `_getche()` and `scanf()`

21.01 Creating and executing the project

Algorithm for Evaluating Postfix Expression

<table>
<tr><td rowspan="6">Evaluating Postfix notation</td><td>decision</td><td colspan="4">take an input for the type of a postfix expression component</td></tr>
<tr><td rowspan="5">process ↻</td><td rowspan="5">proceed according to the input</td><td>decision</td><td colspan="2">the type of a postfix expression component</td></tr>
<tr><td rowspan="4">◆</td><td>';'</td><td>end the repeated process and break</td></tr>
<tr><td>'n'</td><td>take a numerical operand as an input and push the operand to the stack</td></tr>
<tr><td>'o'</td><td>take a operator as an input, pop twice from the stack, and push the result of the calculation to the stack</td></tr>
<tr><td>other</td><td>other cases are input errors</td></tr>
</table>

Practice

* Create the project and execute the project
  - Creating a project
  - Copy stack.cpp, stack.h, postfix.cpp, postfix.h to the project folder and add them as existing items
  - Add main.cpp as a new item and code
  - Run the project by pressing Ctrl+F5 and calculate 11 22 +

KeyPoints

+ Three types of arithmetic expressions

- prefix
- infix
- postfix

+ Operators and operands

- 1 + 2 , 3 4 *
- 1,2,3,4 : operands
- +,* : operators

Output

Practice

※ Execute various test cases

- 1 2 + 3 4 + -
- Enter operands with text characters

    operands : 12A1, 12 2, 12.3, A12
- At the end of an expression, enter '$' instead of ';'
- Enter * or / as an operator

※ Check the result of `scanf()` for the various cases using the debugger

Output

21.02 Understanding scanf(), _getche(), fflush(stdin)

Test Program

```
#include <conio.h>            // required for _getche()
int main(void)
{
   int    digit, ret;
   char   ch, str[128];
   printf("Enter digit : ");
   ret = scanf("%d", &digit);
   printf("\nreturn of scanf : %d, data = %d \n",ret,digit);
   printf("\nEnter char : ");
   ch = _getche();
   printf("\nEnter string : ");
   scanf("%s", str);
   printf("\nstring %s\n", str);
   return 0;
}
```

Practice

Set break points, execute the program in debegging mode, enter test cases below, and trace the value of each variables ([enter] indicates enter key on the keyboard)

※ When fflush(stdin); is not used

- 123 [enter] * abcd [enter]
- 12Aabcd [enter] * abcd [enter]
- A1 [enter] 1 [enter] abcd enter]
- 1 2 [enter] 3 [enter] 4 5 [enter]

Output

KeyPoints

- **scanf() return value:** The number of successfully processed values
- **fflush(stdin):** Removes any unused data from a buffer after scanf()
- **_getche():** Takes a character input directly from keyboard without waiting for an enter key event requires <conio.h>

Practice

※ Call `fflush(stdin);` right after `scanf()`, `_getche()`

▸ Input value with the same order above

Output

21.03 Adding new operators: '*' and '/'

Practice

Expand the program to process multiplication and division operators

* Edit DoOperator() in postfix.cpp
  - Change the prompt message for operator input

    ```
    printf("\tInput +, -, *, / : ");
    ```
  - Add #define MULTIPLY and #define DIVIDE after the #define ADD
  - Edit the code for handling operator inputs(take caution for the division operator)

```
. . .
else
   if (opr == DIVIDE) {
      if (operand2 == 0) {
         printf("\t Cannot divide by 0, ignored \n");
         push(operand1); push(operand2);
      }
      else
          push(operand1 / operand2);
}
```

* Execute the test cases below
  - 1 2 * 1 + 3 *
  - 1 2 - 3 * 4 / 3 4 + *
  - 1 0 /

KeyPoints

+ **Division by 0 causes a program to terminate**
+ **if an if statements becomes too long, use switch() instead:**

  if(x==1) A
  else if (x==2) B
  else if (x==3) C
  . . . is same as
  switch(x) {
  case 1:A; break;
  case 2:B; break;
  case 3:C; break;
  . . .

Output

21.04 Handling the limitations of the stack data structure

◎ Detecting and handling stack overflows and underflows

```
void push(int num)
{
    if (sp >= SIZE) return; // Do not push, to prevent stack overflow
    sp = sp + 1;
    stack[sp] = num;
    return;
}
```

Practice

Edit push() and pop() in stack.cpp to keep the program working even if stack overflows or underflows

✻ Try the cases below to generate stack underflow and overflow

- 1 +
- 1 2 3 4 5 6 7 8 9 10 11 + + + + + + + + + +

✻ Edit #define SIZE to 20 and try the test cases again

✻ Edit the program and execute

- Edit push() and pop()
- Calculate the two cases again

KeyPoints

+ 2 components of stack
- data storage
  stack pointer
- function
  top()
  push()
  pop()

+ push() and overflow

+ pop() and underflow

Output

GUESS??

1) What is the postfix expression for "Add 3 to 2 and multiply the result by 4"?

2) What is the postfix expression for (1 + 2) * (3 - 4)?

3) How can you substitute the words in the sentence below to convert it into an arithmetic notation?

"ADD 1 TO 2"

Ref. Can be expressed as "+ 1 2", which is a prefix notation

4) Calculate 1 2 3 4 5 6 + − − − + using stack

5) Why do people use these various complex notations for arithmetic expressions? What are the advantages and disadvantages of these notations?

6) Do we need parentheses in postfix expressions?

7) Think of some problems that can be solved more conveniently by using stack.

Project 22

Evaluating Infix Expression

Project Description

Write a program that evaluates infix expressions with operators '+', '-', '*', and '/', which are of same precedence and left-associative. Operands can be either numbers or character strings.

- When ';' is entered as an input, the program outputs the result of evaluation and terminates.
- The program recognizes '+', '-', '*', and '/' as operators. Numbers and character strings are recognized as operators.

```
C:\Windows\system32\cmd.exe
Welcome to infix expression evaluation
 list of symbols
------------------------------
          a      1
          b      2
         ab      3
        abc      4
------------------------------
Enter operator(+,-,*,/), value, or ; : 1
Enter operator(+,-,*,/), value, or ; : +
Enter operator(+,-,*,/), value, or ; : 2
Enter operator(+,-,*,/), value, or ; : -
Enter operator(+,-,*,/), value, or ; : 3
Enter operator(+,-,*,/), value, or ; : +
Enter operator(+,-,*,/), value, or ; : 4
Enter operator(+,-,*,/), value, or ; : ;
Value of expression : 4
Press any key to continue . . .
```

Main Concepts

Symbol table

Symbol table refers to a data structure where the names of symbols used in a program are mapped to their attributes, as names of friends are mapped to their phone numbers in a contact list. Names of symbols corresponds to names of friends, and phone numbers or addresses of friends corresponds to attributes of symbols.

Main Objectives

- Writing codes with the top-down approach
- Evaluating infix expressions
- Programming and using symbol tables(`typedef` and `struct`)
- Precedence and associativity
- Character to number conversion such as `atoi()`, `atof()`

22.01 Creating and executing a project

⑥ Coding main using abstraction

Repeating input process of infix expression components	Decision	After ';' is entered, break out of the iteration process
	Process	Process operators
		Process operands
Outputs the result of evaluation		

Evaluating infix expressions with operators of same precedence and left-associativity

- Calculate when an operand is entered after an operator
- Therefore, an expression can be evaluated immediately after the second operand is entered

Ref. This method cannot be used if the precedence or associativity of operators change

Practice

* Create the project and code
  - Copy symbolTable.cpp, symbolTable.h, infix.cpp, infix.h to the project folder and add them as existing items
  - Add main.cpp as a new item and code
    - #include header files
    - Declare variables (e.g. char in[INLEN])
    - When writing main.cpp, use top-down approach

* Simple evaluations
  - 1 + 2 - 3 + 4 ;
  - 1 + a - b * ab ;

Output

KeyPoints

- **top-down approach to writing code**
  - top : caller
  - down : callee
- **Abstraction**
  - top : what-to-do
  - down : how-to-do
- **prototype is required to use functions before declarations**
- **Because of equal precedence and left-associativity, the value of 1 + 2 * 3 is 9, not 7**

22.02 Understanding **atoi()**, **atof()**, **scanf()**, **gets()**

⑥ Testing Main Functionalities

```
#include <stdio.h>
#include <stdlib.h>
int main(void)
{
    int    digit, ret, k;
    char   str[128];
    printf("Enter digit string : ");
    ret = scanf("%s", str);
    printf("Echo = %s, return of scanf = %d \n", str, ret);
    digit = atoi(str);
    printf("atoi(%s) = %d \n", str, digit);
    return 0;
}
```

Practice

※ Write the program above and execute the test cases below

- 123
- 12.34
- -12
- 12 34
- 12ab

Output

KeyPoints

- **atoi(str) : A function that converts a string str to an integer value**
  atoi("2014")=2014
- **atof() : Converts a string to a float**
- **gets() : A function that reads a line of input. In other words, reads until an enter key event. Accepts space events.**
- **scanf() return value**
  The number of successfully proccessed items

Practice

* Edit `scanf("%s", str);` and execute
  - `scanf("%s\n", str);`
  - `scanf("%s", str);`

* Replace `scanf("%s", str);` with `gets(str);` and execute the cases above again

* Replace `atoi()` with `atof()` and execute

* Reading multiple variable values with one `scanf()`
  - `ret = scanf("%d%d", &digit, &k);`
    `printf("ret of scanf = %d, digit = %d\n", ret, digit);`
  - Enter 1A

Output

22.03 Understanding symbol table

◎ Symbol table implementation

A symbol table is an array of symbols, and a symbol consists of a name and a value.

concept	implementation
A symbol table is an array of symbols	`#define MAXSYMBOLS 3` `SYMBOL symbolTable [MAXSYMBOLS];`

A symbol consists of a name and a value	`typedef struct {`
	`char name [NAMELEN];`
	`int value ;`
	`} SYMBOL;`

Initialization method	`SYMBOL symbolTable [MAXSYMBOLS] =` `{ {"a", 1}, {"b", 2}, {"ab", 3} };`

Practice

* Add a new symbol "abc" with value 4 to the symbolTable.cpp
  - Adding symbols to a symbol table
    - Extend the size of the array
      `#define MAXSYMBOLS 4`
    - add `{"abc", 4}` to the initialization

* Calculate these expressions by executing in debugging mode
  - 1 * ab - abc ;
  - 1 * abc - abcd ;
  - 1 % abc ;
  - * 1 ;

KeyPoints

+ typedef :
A user defines a data type. SYMBOL is used as a data type such as int or float.

+ typedef int INT;
INT k; is same as int k;

+ struct :
Allows the binding of two or more data together.

Output

22.04 Evaluating Infix Expressions with Float Operands

Practice

Edit the program to accept float operands and execute the program

* Edit the program to reflect the data type change
  - Edit main.cpp
    - `printf("…%3.1f\n", value);`
  - Edit the type of variable 'value' in infix.cpp
    - Change the type of 'value' to `float`
    - Change the return type of `GetInfixExpValue()` to `float`
    - Change the types in `EvaluateExp()` to `float`
    - Edit the type of `symValue` in `DoInfixOperand()`
  - Edit the prototypes in infix.h
  - Edit symbolTable.cpp
    - Change the type of 'value', which is a member variable of `symbolTable[]`, to `float`
    - Change the return type of `GetSymbolValue()` to `float`
    - Change the `%d` in `printf()` to `%3.1f`
    - Edit all the initialization values e.g. 1.0, 2.0, 3.0
  - Edit the prototypes in symbolTable.h

KeyPoints

- in printf, 3.1f outputs only one digit after the decimal point
- In a program where typedef int VTP; is declared and VTP is used in place of int, declaring typedef float VTP; modifies the program to handle float values without having to change anything else

Output

Practice

※ Execute test cases below

- 1.1 + 2.2 ;

※ Utilizing a header file with `typedef int tVALUE;`

- Add infixtype.h as a new item
  - `typedef int  tVALUE;`
  - `#define SYMTBLPRTFORMAT    "%10s   %3d\n"`
- Add `#include "infixtype.h"` to all .cpp files
- Add initialization of tValue in symbolTable.cpp, e.g. `(tValue) 1`
- Edit print in `main()` to %d, or `%.2f`, according to the type
- Only infixtype.h is required to be edited

Output

GUESS??

1) If operators have different precedence, evaluations cannot be done right after an operand is entered. Think about the evaluation of 1 + 2 * 3. 1 + 2 cannot be evaluated immediately after 2 is entered. How should this expression be evaluated?

2) In postfix expressions, precedence was not taken into consideration. If operators have equal precedence, 1+2*3 in postfix expression is 1 2+3*. On the other hand, if '*' has higher precedence than '+', the postfix expression is 1 2 3*+.

3) An array saves multiple values in one allotted memory space, so does a structure(`struct`). What is the difference between two concepts?

4) `typedef` is a widely-used method of defining user-defined types. what are the advantages of using `typedef`? What are the disadvantages?

Project 23

The Coding Strategy for Troubleshooting

Finite State Machine and Token Parsing

Project Description

Write a program that splits an infix expression using tokens and outputs the results.

- Numbers, alphabets(upper and lowercase), operators('+', '-', '*', '/', ';')
- Any other characters are considered as tokens

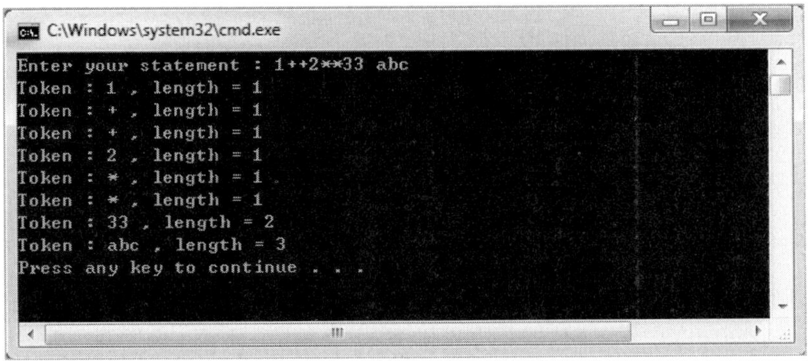

Main Concepts

Finite Automata

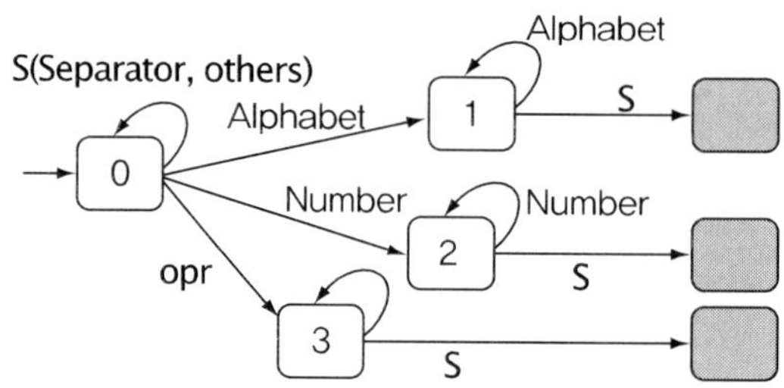

Finite State Machine(FSM)

`int FSM [S_SIZE] [IN_TYPE]`

	input				
	num	alfa	operator	sep	others
S_START	S_NUMBER	S_SYMBOL	S_OPERATOR	S_START	S_START
S_SYMBOL	-1	S_SYMBOL	-1	-1	-1
S_NUMBER	S_NUMBER	-1	-1	-1	-1
S_OPERATOR	-1	-1	-1	-1	-1

Main Objectives

- ✎ Writing codes with the top-down approach
- ✎ Model-based coding techniques
- ✎ Understanding token and scanner
- ✎ Understanding and utilizing `static`, `extern` variables
- ✎ `gets()` implementation

23.01 Creating and executing the project

⑥ The top-down approach for coding main

<table>
<tr><td colspan="3">Entering infix expression</td></tr>
<tr><td colspan="3">Initializing token parsing</td></tr>
<tr><td rowspan="2">Parse each token, and out put the parsed token</td><td>Decision</td><td>Parse a token
If there is no more token to be parsed, break out of the iteration process</td></tr>
<tr><td>Process</td><td>Output the token and the length of the token</td></tr>
</table>

Practice

* Create the project and code
  - Copy scanner.cpp, scanner.h to the project folder and add as existing items
  - Add main.cpp as a new item and code
    - #include header files, #define INLEN
    - Declare variables (char in[INLEN];)
      Do not define token and tokenlen, which are defined extern, in scanner.h(including header files takes care of it)
    - Write main()

* Execute simple test cases
  - 1 + 2 - 3 + 4 ;
  - 1 + a - b * ab ;
  - 1++2**33 abc ;
  - 1 + ab - abc ;
  - 1#$%abc123 +cd

KeyPoints

+ scanner
A program that parses tokens

+ Header file
Declares extern variables, types, and function prototypes in .cpp files as shown below

```
#ifndef
   __name_H_
#define
   __name_H_
<declare>
#endif
```

+ gets(char in[])
Used for reading a character string line with empty spaces untill '\n' appears

Output

23.02 Understanding table implementation of FSM

◎ Understanding the FSM table

	state ID	input (arrow)	
		alfa(alphabet)	etc
	0		
curstate	1	nextstate = 1	-1
(won)	. . .		

State Transition

```
while(1) {
    . . .
    curstate = nextstate;
    nextstate = FSM[curstate][input];
    . . .
}
```

Practice

＊ Understanding the algorithm using debugger

- Set a break point at NextToken() in scanner.cpp
- Execute the program in debugging mode(F5)

  Enter 1 + a23 ++ bcd ;
- Add relevant variables to the watch window
- Take single steps until the program termination(check the values in the watch window)

KeyPoints

+ FSM

- column : state behaviour
- row : type of input

+ Model-based programming

- By modelling FSM as a table first, the code becomes more formulated and organized
- By editing the array, new types of tokens can be parsed(e.g.) Allowing symbols with numbers after an alphabet

Output

Practice

※ Test the result of editing FSM table

- Change the value of `FSM[1][0]` (`stateID = S_SYMBOL`, `input = num`) to `S_SYMBOL`
- Execute the program in debugging mode, and enter 1 + a23 ++ bcd ;
- Trace the token parsing process

Output

23.03 Adding new token types(expanding the FSM table)

⑥ FSM table expansion to recognize floats(e.g.: 12.34) as a token

`int FSM [S_SIZE] [IN_TYPE]`

	input					
	num	alfa	operator	sep	others	period
S_START	S_NUMBER	S_SYMBOL	S_OPERATOR	S_START	S_START	S_FLOAT
S_SYMBOL	-1	S_SYMBOL	-1	-1	-1	-1
S_NUMBER	S_NUMBER	-1	-1	-1	-1	S_FLOAT
S_OPERATOR	-1	-1	-1	-1	-1	-1
S_FLOAT	S_FLOAT	-1	-1	-1	-1	-1

- If a decimal point .(period) appears after numbers, enter the `float` state(S_FLOAT)

  Impl. A new column(period) and a row(S_FLOAT) are added

- In S_FLOAT(after period), only numbers are allowed

  Impl. Only `FSM[S_FLOAT][num]`is S_FLOAT

Practice

✻ Expand FSM for period, S_FLOAT(refer to the description above)

- Edit `CharType()` to recognize period('.')
- Expand the size of FSM(increase the number of rows and columns)
- Fill the FSM

✻ Trace token parsing process using debugging mode

- 3.5 + 6.7 * a;
- 1.2.3.4 - 2.3.4.5

KeyPoints

+ Diagram

- FSM in a form of graph

+ Token recognization / processing

- If the next state becomes −1, it indicates the end of the token being scanned
- Developers can specify a special values for special processing

Output

23.04 Lifetime and accessibility of **extern**, **static** variables

Types of main.cpp, f.cpp, f.h

(1) main.cpp	(2) main.cpp	(3) f.cpp

#include <stdio.h>
#include "f.h"
int main(void)
{
  f();
 	
printf("%d\n",value);
}
	#include <stdio.h>
	#include "f.h"
	int value = 10;
	int main(void)
	{
	  f();
	
	printf("%d\n",value);
	}
		int value =100;
		void f(void)
		{
		  value++;
		}

(4) f.h	**(5) f.h**	**(6) f.cpp**

#ifndef __F_H_
#define __F_H_
extern int value;
void f(void);
#endif
	#ifndef __F_H_
	#define __F_H_
	void f(void);
	#endif
		static int value =100;
		void f(void)
		{
		  value++;
		}

Practice

* Create a project with following combinations of main.cpp, f.cpp, f.h and execute the program
  - (1) + (3) + (4)
  - (2) + (3) + (4)
  - (1) + (3) + (5)
  - (2) + (3) + (5)
  - (1) + (6) + (4)
  - (2) + (6) + (4)
  - (1) + (6) + (5)
  - (2) + (6) + (5)

KeyPoints

+ **storage class**
  - auto
  - static
  - extern
+ **extern**
  - lifetime of values: maintained
  - accessibility: global
+ **static**
  - lifetime of values: maintained
  - accessibility: limited

Output

GUESS??

1) FSM is a popular modelling technique. What are some of the problems(or systems) that can be modelled using FSM?

2) What are the advantage of a diagram over a table?

3) Express the behaviour of turnstile with a table.

4) In `a++` or `a--;`, ++ and -- are operators. In FSM from chapter 23, they are recognized as two tokens. Edit the FSM to recognize ++ as a single token.

5) Currently, scanner.cpp is required to be edited if FSM is modified. It is possible to design scanner.cpp so that FSM can be modified without editing `StartScanning()` and `NextToken()`. How should you reconstruct the project?

Project 24

The Coding Strategy for Troubleshooting

Implementing BNF Parser

Project Description

Write a program that parses a grammar file, which specifies one rule per line, and outputs the result as shown below. Check if each rule follows BNF format and point out errors.

an example of grammar file

```
<sentence> ::= <subject> <verb>
<subject> ::= <noun>
<noun> ::= Tom
<verb> ::= hate
```

```
Enter the name of the grammar file : grammar.txt

** RULE TABLE **
   1     2     3
   1     2     3     4
   2     5
   2     6
   4     5
   5     7
   5     8
   6     9
   6    10
   3    11
   3    12
   3    13
```

```
** TOKEN TABLE **

 NON-TERMINAL
[    1] <sentence>
[    2] <subject>
[    3] <verb>
[    4] <object>
[    5] <noun>
[    6] <pronoun>

 TERMINAL
[    7] Tom
[    8] Jerry
[    9] I
[   10] You
[   11] love
[   12] like
[   13] hate
Press any key to continue . . .
```

Main Concepts

BNF(BACKUS NAUR FORM)

An example of simple english grammar in BNF

```
<sentence> ::= <noun> <verb>
<sentence> ::= <noun> <verb> <noun>
<noun>     ::= Jerry
<noun>     ::= Mom
<verb>     ::= love
```

grammar

Terms

- Non-terminal symbols
  <sentence>, <noun>, <verb>
- Terminal symbols
  Jerry, Mom, love

Main Objectives

✎ Coding with the top-down approach
✎ String operations
✎ Implementation of scanner using `sscanf()`
✎ File input/output

24.01 Completing the program using top-down approach

Flow and structure of the program

- `main`
  - ✓ Parses grammar file rules
  - ✓ Outputs the result of the parsing
- Grammar file parsing
  - ✓ repeatedly parse the grammar rules in each line
- Parsing of each rule
  - ✓ Repeating these process
    - token extraction
    - saving the extracted token to the table
  - ✓ Adding the new rule to the rule table

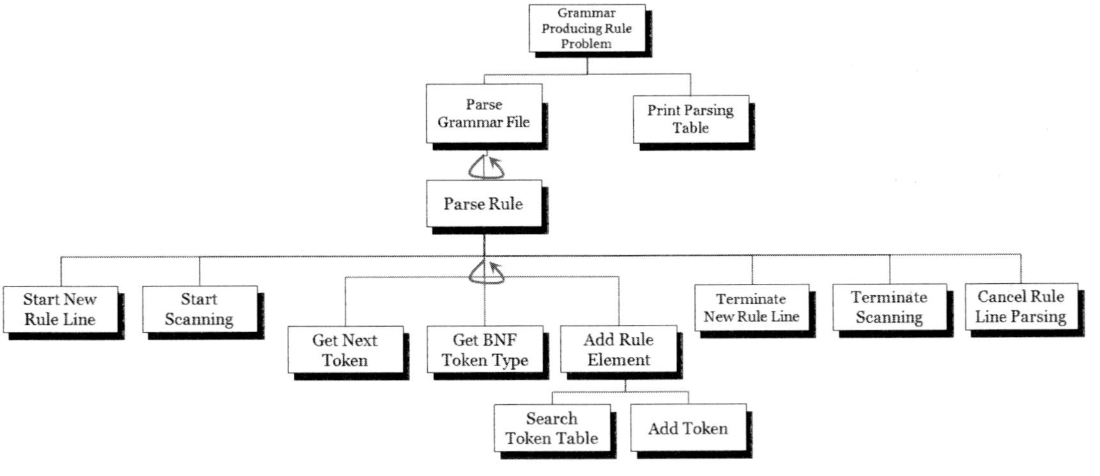

Practice

Create an empty project, follow the steps below to complete and execute

* Add .cpp, .h files specified in the design to the project as new/existing items

* Add main.cpp as a new item and start writing code
  - #include header files for the required modules in main()

```
#include "GramFile.h"
#include "parseTable.h"
```

  - code main() according to the logic(refer to the description above)

* Code GramFile.cpp
  - refer to the files provided
  - Code bool parseGrammarFile(char *gramfile)
    - Prepare the file for use; // fopen()
    - while(1) { ParseRuleLine(); } // Parse rule lines
    - Close the file; // fclose()
  - Code int ParseRuleLine(char rule[])
    - Implement BNF rule structure "<non-terminal> := row of tokens"

* Code parseTable.cpp and scanner.cpp

* Copy grammar.txt to the project, execute and check the output of the program

KeyPoints

+ Module
- Component of a program
- Implemented as an independent file

+ Structure chart
- A figure depicting the relationship between modules

+ top-down
- An approch of writing code, starting from the top of the structure chart and continuing downward

Output

24.02 Token splitting using **strtok()**

⑥ **strtok()** Test Program

```
If space(" ") is the delimiters for grammar rules, use strtok()
#define SPR " \t\n"         // The first character is space
int main()
{
   char  in[256], *token;
   printf("Enter rule : ");
   gets(in);
   token = strtok(in, SPR);
   while(1) {
      if (token==NULL) break;
      printf("token = %s, length =%d\n", token, strlen(token));
      token = strtok(NULL, SPR);
   }
   return 0;
}
```

Practice

Check the outputs of the program for following inputs

- <sentence> ::= <noun> <verb>
- sentence> ::= <noun> <verb>
- <sentence space ::= <noun> <verb>
- <noun   > ::= Jerry
- <noun>   ::= 'Tom   '
- <sentence> ::= <noun> loves what he knows

KeyPoints

+ strtok()

- The first call of strok
  strtok(str, SPR);
- After the first call
  strtok(NULL, SPR);
  SPR is the token delimiter
  (e.g.) space, tab or newline character
  SPR = " \t\n"

Output

24.03 Implementing myStrtok()

Implementing **myStrtok()** using static variables

```
char * myStrtok(char *input, char *separator)
{
   static char *cursor = NULL, *end;
   char        *ret;
   if (input != NULL) {
      cursor = input;       // only set the cursor for the first call
      end = &cursor[strlen(input)];
   }
   if (cursor == NULL || cursor == end) return NULL;
   while (cursor<end && NullOrSep(*cursor, separator)==true)
      *(cursor++) = '\0';
   ret = cursor;
   while (cursor<=end && NullOrSep(*cursor, separator)==false)
      cursor++;
   *cursor = '\0';
   if (ret == cursor) ret = NULL;
   return ret;
}
```

Practice

* In strtok() test program, replace strtok() with myStrtoK() and test myStrtoK() using lines below(but, NullOrSep(char ch, char *separator); requires coding)

- <sentence> ::= <noun> <verb>
- sentence> ::= <noun> <verb>
- <sentence> ::= <noun> loves what he knows
- <sentence> ::= you know all of what you love

Output

KeyPoints

+ static
- The value is maintained after the function is finished

+ pointer / array name
- The usages are the same
- Only array declaration secures memory space

+ *(ptr++);
- Finds the value pointed by ptr, and increment ptr by 1
- Different from (*ptr)++;

Practice

✻ Use the debugger to analyze myStrtok()

- Set a break point at `if (input!=NULL)` in `myStrtok()`
- Start debugging by pressing F5
- Put `*cursor` and `ret` in the watch window
- Proceed in `myStrtok()` using F10

Output

24.04 Understanding File IO and standard stream(**stdin**, **stdout**, **stderr**)

⑨ File IO functions **fscanf()**, **fprintf()**, **fgets()** and **stdin/stdout/stderr**

```
#include <stdio.h>
int main (void)
{
   FILE  *fp;
   int    n;
   char   line[256];
   if((fp = fopen("exampleFILEIO.txt", "w")) == NULL) {      // STEP1
      printf("Cannot create file exampleFILEIO.txt \n");
      return 0;
   }
   for (n = 0; n < 5; n++) {
      printf("enter a name : ");
      gets(line);
      fprintf(fp,"Line %3d:[%s]\n", n, line);                // STEP 2
   }
   fclose(fp);                                               // STEP 3
   return 0;
}
```

Practice

* Testing fopen(), fprintf(), fclose()
  - Code the program above
  - Execute the program and check the output "exampleFILEIO.txt" with the windows notepad
  - Replace `fprintf(fp,"Line %3d:[%s]\n", n, line);` with `fprintf(stdout,"Line %3d:[%s]\n", n, line);`

KeyPoints

+ **file operation procedure**
  - fopen()
  - fprintf()/fgets()
  - fclose()
+ **fgets() and gets()**
  - Similar but different
  - gets() removes '\n'
+ **fgets()**
  - reads '\n'
  - If fgets() is called at the eof(end of file), it returns null
  - fscanf() replaces '\n' with '\0'

Output

Practice

* Edit the program and execute in debugging mode to check the character at the end of the line

```
if((fp = fopen("exampleFILEIO.txt", "r")) == NULL)
...
while(1) {
   if (fgets(line, 256, fp) == NULL) break;
      printf("%s\n", line);  // Output displays an
                             // additional empty line
}
fclose(fp);
```

Output

24.05 Implementing grammar rule scanner using **sscanf()**

int sscanf (char *input, char*format, void **pointer*, *void* * *pointer*, . . .)

Scans *input* according to the *format*(conversion specifications), and saves the result at the addresses pointed by the pointer

FORMAT	Input example	sscanf call format
"%d %s %d"	12 abc 34	ret = sscanf(line, FORMAT1, &v1, str, &v2);
"<%[^>]>"	<programs>	ret = sscanf(line, FORMAT2, str);
"%*c%[0-9]"	$123	ret = sscanf(line, FORMAT3, str);
"%[0-9A-Za-z]"	0123abAB	ret = sscanf(line, FORMAT4, str);
"ID:%d"	ID:123	ret = sscanf(line, FORMAT5, &v1);
"%[^ \t>]"	123	ret = sscanf(line, FORMAT6, str);

```
#define FORMAT1 "%d %s %d"
int main(void)
{
   int v1, v2, ret;
   char line[512], str[512] = { 0 };  // str must be initialized
   printf("input formnat %s :", FORMAT1);
   gets(line);
   ret = sscanf(line, FORMAT1, &v1, str, &v2);
   printf("sscanf retruns %d, v1=[%5d], v2=[%5d], str=[%s]\n", ret, v1,
          v2, str);
}
```

Practice

※ Understanding `sscanf` by using various inputs for each format

- Using inputs with string that conforms to the format
- Using inputs with string that does not conform to the format
- Points of observation
  - The return value for `sscanf()`, `ret`
  - The value from `sscanf()`

※ The result of calling `sscanf()` without initializing str first with `str[] = {0};`

KeyPoints

- examples format usage
- %[a-z] strings with lowercase alphabet
- %[^>] string befor >, excludes the string after ^
- %*c ignores one character

Output

24.06 Understanding grammar file parsing

Practice

Tracing file parsing and error handling

※ Use the debugger to trace file parsing procedure

- Set a break point at the first line of the function `ParseRuleLine()`
- Execute the program in debugging mode, use F11 to proceed and check the values of variables

※ Error handling

- Handling grammar error in `ParseRuleLine()`

```
if (StartRuleLine() < 0)            goto PARSE_ERROR;
if (StartScanning(rule) < 0)        goto PARSE_ERROR;
   . . .
   return 0;  // indicates normal termination
PARSE_ERROR:  // if the error occurs the program jumps
              // to here
   CancelRuleLineParsing();
   return -1;
```

KeyPoints

High reliability program - prepare for

- exceptional cases
- overflow
- input errors

goto <label>;

- Makes the program 'jump' to another place
- Limited uses of goto can simplify code
- Notice the ':' after the label

Output

Practice

- Handling table overflow in parseTable.cpp

```
if (rule_no >= MAX_RULE - 1 . . . ) // rule overflow
   return -1;
```

or

```
if (token_no >= MAX_TOKEN - 1)      // token overflow
   return -1;
```

※ Test using various error cases

- Errors in grammar.txt
  - Non-terminal cases without '<' or '>'
  - Missing :=
- If the size of rule_table or token_table is too small
  - If the grammar file has too many rules
  - If there are too many terminal or non-terminal symbols

Output

GUESS??

1) Is "::=" a token or not?

2) What is the rule for generating sentences like "I Love You"? If 〈subject〉 was used to define this rule, is 〈subject〉 a non-terminal symbol or a terminal symbol?

3) How can you define 〈pronoun〉 as YOU? is YOU a non-terminal symbol or a terminal symbol?

5) Can you describe a part of your daily life with grammar using BNF?

6) What is the BNF diagram?

Project 25

Console Input / Output

Project Description

Write a program that reads input from specific places on a screen or outputs the string with different colors.

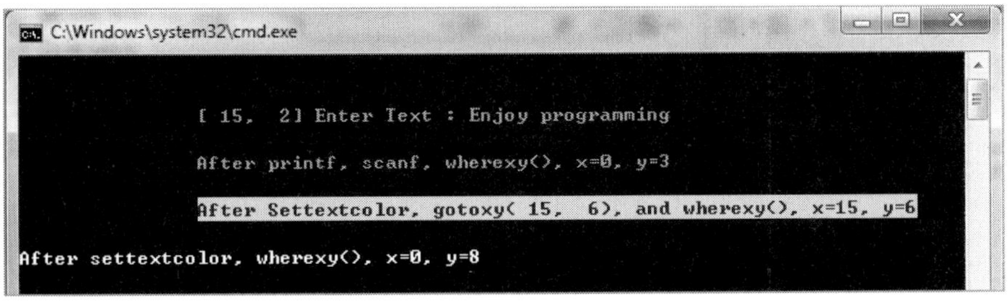

Main Concepts

console IO

- `printf("\n")`, `scanf()` reads and outputs at the next line, and the color is fixed
- It is possible to change colors or specify places of input/output
- Notable colors

```
typedef enum { BLACK, GRAY = 7, DGRAY, BLUE, GREEN, SKY, RED,
                    YELLOW = 14, WHITE } WINCOLSOLECOLOR;
```

Main Objectives

✎ Controlling the console screen

✎ Coordinate system of the console screen (x : horizontal, y : vertical)

✎ `enum` type

✎ Passing arguments of functions

25.01 Controlling console output location in windows

Setting input/output cursor position or checking the current cursor position

```
#include "winconio.h"
#define  OUTPUTHANDLE  GetStdHandle(STD_OUTPUT_HANDLE)
void gotoxy(int x, int y)
{
   COORD p = { x, y };
   HANDLE h = OUTPUTHANDLE;
   if (h == INVALID_HANDLE_VALUE)  return;
   SetConsoleCursorPosition(h, p);
}
void wherexy(int *x, int *y)
{
   CONSOLE_SCREEN_BUFFER_INFO BufInfo;
   HANDLE h = OUTPUTHANDLE;
   if (h == INVALID_HANDLE_VALUE) return;
   GetConsoleScreenBufferInfo(h, &BufInfo);
   *x = BufInfo.dwCursorPosition.X;
   *y = BufInfo.dwCursorPosition.Y;
}
```

Practice

Test for understanding the functionality of the above functions

※ Create an empty project, copy and add winconio.cpp and winconio.h

※ Add and code main.cpp

```
#include <stdio.h>
#include "winconio.h"
int main()
{
    int row, col;
    // Call combinations of gotoxy(), wherexy(),
       printf(), scanf()
    // Write the example below, refer to wherexy()
       description
    // wherexy(&col,&row);
    // printf("x=col=%d, y=row=%d\n",col,row);
}
```

※ '&' operator functionality

- Delete '&' from `wherexy(&col, &row)` and test the function
- Test `printf("row = %d, &row = %d\n", row, &row);`

KeyPoints

- **&variable: address of the variable**
  - &row : the address where the value of row is stored
  - When calling the function, pass as &row, but in the function definition, use int * to process
- **COORD**

```
typedef struct {
    int  X;
    int  Y;
} COORD;
```

- **COORD p ={x,y};**

Output

25.02 Changing background or text colors

⊚ Changing the color of background or text

```
#include "winconio.h"
void settextcolor(int color, int bgcolor)      // changing text color
{
    color &= 0xf;
    bgcolor &= 0xf;
    HANDLE h = OUTPUTHANDLE;
    if (h == INVALID_HANDLE_VALUE) return;
    SetConsoleTextAttribute(h, (bgcolor << 4 | color));
}
void  gettextcolor(int *color, int *bgcolor)   // getting text color
{
    CONSOLE_SCREEN_BUFFER_INFO info;
    HANDLE h = OUTPUTHANDLE;
    if (h == INVALID_HANDLE_VALUE) return;
    GetConsoleScreenBufferInfo(h, &info);
    *color = info.wAttributes & 0xf;
    *bgcolor = (info.wAttributes & 0xf0) >> 4;
}
```

Practice

※ In main() of the previous project, add statements to call the functions

※ Testing colors of background and text

- Use various colors of `WINCONSOLECOLOR` as parameters for `settextcolor()`
- Test the values from 0 to 15 and check the output colors

※ Output the values for each colors

```
printf(" BLACK = %d n", BLACK);
printf(" DGRAY = %d n", DGRAY);
printf(" SKY   = %d n", SKY); . . .
```

KeyPoints

+ typedef enum {
BLACK,
GRAY = 7,
DGRAY,
BLUE,
GREEN,
SKY,
RED,
YELLOW = 14,
WHITE}
WINCOLSOLECOLOR;
Find the values of each color in the enum definition

+ It is easier to read/write program using BLUE instead of numbers

Output

25.03 Applications of other functions

⑥ Additional functions

```
#define  MINSIZE   10
void getMaxConsole()
{
   HANDLE    h = OUTPUTHANDLE;
   COORD     largest;
   COORD     windowSize;
   SMALL_RECT       info;

   if (h == INVALID_HANDLE_VALUE) return;
   largest = GetLargestConsoleWindowSize(h);
   windowSize = { largest.X, largest.Y };
   if (largest.X <= MINSIZE || largest.Y <= MINSIZE) return;
   info = {0, 0, windowSize.X - MINSIZE, windowSize.Y - MINSIZE};
   SetConsoleScreenBufferSize(h, largest);
   if (!SetConsoleWindowInfo(h, TRUE, &info)) return;
}
```

Practice

Continue using the previous project

* Code main.cpp to generate the output screen in the problem description
* Maximizing the console window
  * Call `getMaxConsole()`
* Search for other functions and their use on google
  * After finding other functions, write code for them and execute the program
* Make some function calls into comments from `getMaxConsole()` and execute the program

KeyPoints

+ Other functions

Windows provides various functions for controlling the console window

Output

GUESS??

1) What is the advantage of using enum types over using integers?

2) What are the errors in **wherexy()** usages below?

(1)
```
int  row, col;
wherexy(row, col);
```

(2)
```
int  *row, *col;
wherexy(&row, &col);
```

(3)
```
int  *row = NULL, *col=NULL;
wherexy(row, col);
```

3) What causes the errors when you use **wherexy()** as shown below?

```
void wherexy(int *x, int *y)
{
   CONSOLE_SCREEN_BUFFER_INFO BufInfo;
   GetConsoleScreenBufferInfo(OUTPUTHANDLE, &BufInfo);
   x = BufInfo.dwCursorPosition.X;
   y = BufInfo.dwCursorPosition.Y;
}
```

Index

The Coding Strategy
for Troubleshooting